Raymond Oursel
Henri Stierlin (Ed.)

# Romanesque

Photos: Jacques Rouiller
Preface: Hermann Baur

Benedikt Taschen

| | |
|---|---|
| Editor of Series | Henri Stierlin |
| Plans | Jean Duret FAS SIA |
| **English Translation** | **Kenneth Martin Leake** |

# Contents

3    Preface: The Heritage of Romanesque Genius

7    Introduction: The Approaches

47    1.  Background to Romanesque

85    2.  The Builders

127    3.  Impulses and Themes

173    4.  Unity of Vision

185    Chronological Table

189    Bibliography

191    Table of Contents

# The Heritage of Romanesque Genius

Preface by Hermann Baur

The communication of modern architecture with that of the past is a characteristic unknown to our predecessors. Up to the nineteenth century architects paid little attention to earlier periods and openly sought some style that differed from them. They automatically thought of the period before theirs as a starting point from which they could penetrate the unknown. This is particularly so in the case of Romanesque art. Little survives of Glaber's 'white mantle of churches' which covered the West after the year 1000. The Gothic period which followed either suppressed or forgot the Romanesque.

The advent of the age of historical investigation led to a modification of this state of intuitive creation. There began a static period of reflection which found its outward expression in Neoclassicism. Ancient Greece was set up as an ideal and its buildings were made the scale of architectural values. This point of view, with its almost exclusive exaltation of classical taste, held sway until the time of Jacob Burckhardt. It followed that medieval buildings, and Romanesque architecture especially, were considered primitive and ignoble and, therefore, shunned.

The Romantic Movement which flourished at the beginning of the nineteenth century was a revolt against this lack of interest. Its followers began afresh to seek out and cherish what the Neoclassicists had spurned. They rediscovered the irrational innocence and grotesque imaginativeness of Romanesque architecture and sculpture. The result of this, however, was a fresh attachment to the past. Romanesque, along with Gothic, was considered the religious style 'par excellence' and was recommended by the ecclesiastical authorities for new churches right up to the twentieth century. We are now well aware of the fatal consequences of this conception for the creative forces of art.

It was left to the new architecture of the early

twentieth century to clarify our relations with the art of the past, insisting on knowledge but not imitation. We have learnt to view earlier artistic glories against their complex historical backgrounds. Moreover, we are aware of their imperishable qualities and of the extent to which they remained incomplete, so that our own age may perhaps form a continuation for them.

The needs and possibilities of contemporary architecture are quite different. Modern techniques have modified the problems of building construction. Belief in God which encouraged the Romanesque world is no longer a significant feature of our world. Churches no longer dominate our cities and our countryside. The age of great cathedrals and vast monasteries is over. Nevertheless, there is no doubt a particular affinity between modern architecture and Romanesque art, though this is difficult to explain. It is distinguished by a predilection for the clear, simple forms which are so apparent in small Romanesque churches.

Choir of the church of St Nicholas, Birsfelden, by Hermann Baur

Church porch at Döttingen, by Hermann Baur

All Saints Church, Basle, by Hermann Baur. A surprising resemblance to a Romanesque altar.

It is highly instructive to compare some of our new churches or designs for churches with Romanesque buildings, particularly those in France. Among the points of resemblance between our own age and the Romanesque we may note the theme of the 'portal' which has now taken on a renewed importance, whereas to the Romanesque architects it was both significant and novel. Again, there is the surprising resemblance between Romanesque and modern altars, both expressing the idea of a communion table with direct simplicity. The contemporary trend to integrate sculpture and painting with architecture is also typical of the Romanesque. This integration may be found in buildings whose raw concrete walls are marked with finely drawn lines or motifs in relief. Nor is there any doubt as to the relationship of modern and Romanesque paintings in their common denial of naturalism and their tendency to abstraction.

A thousand years separates our age from the era which saw the Romanesque expand in its portrayal of a new universe through its buildings and its imagery. Over this period the resources of mankind have changed beyond all imagining, affording us the subjection of natural forces and completely new conditions of life. Nevertheless, despite the changes to the face of the world over the centuries, we still build bridges towards a past which is at once so distant and so close. We live in our own troubled period; we strive to give it a worthwhile image in the pattern of history and gratefully subscribe to the tokens left us by the Romanesque. We contemplate the work of their architects with admiration and return to our own moved and enriched by their intelligence.

Romanesque churches derive basically from the Roman basilica, but they abandoned this plan in favor of entirely new spatial forms and constructional systems directly related to Christian ritual. The transepts which cut the nave and the additional height of the crossing denoting the space for the altar are clear indications of this. Small Romanesque churches with their interiors focussing on the altar space are especially relevant.

Indeed, here resides the attraction of something which the religious architecture of our own time is especially eager to attain: a spatial form answering almost exactly to what a church ought to be and ought to give. Just as in the early eleventh century, we are ridding ourselves of outmoded conventions in favor of a revived conception of the church.

Basle, 1966

# The Approaches

Enthusiasm for the wonders of Romanesque civilization is comparatively recent. In the Middle Ages, churches scarcely fifty years old were demolished so that larger, more beautiful cathedrals could be built on their sites. These rest on the foundations of their predecessors, usually incorporating no more than their crypts – sad witnesses of the architectural forms supplanted by the taste of the new era. This prolific expansion has deprived us for ever of some of the foremost architectural expressions in history. In addition, the financial extremes of the early fourteenth century, the dramatic events which shook the western world in the reign of Philip the Fair, economic depression, and, finally, a European war with its accompanying wake of destruction, helped to put an end to this flowering. No one was ashamed to witness this profanation, no one shrank from the destruction of time-honored ordinances. Poverty, disregard and contempt of tradition rather than respect for it, breed and maintain conservatism.

## A legacy threatened and betrayed

In the final years of the fifteenth century, the world shook off the rags of disease and war which had been throttling it for over a century; it embraced fresh illusions and rejected as barbaric and unworthy of revival those which only yesterday it had approved. The contemptuous label of 'Gothic' was applied at random to Romanesque treasuries, French cathedrals, great abbey churches and humble country sanctuaries. Localization of taste and imitation of the antique, which was laid down as a dogma, diverted patrons from religious building. In the sixteenth century more castles than churches were built, and this did not apply only to the Loire valley.

The religious wars launched the severest blow against this unappreciated heritage. It is by no means an understatement that, throughout

Europe, from the Pyrenees to the valleys of Bohemia, extant churches have been sadly marked by outbreaks of fanatical destruction. On the other hand, anyone visiting a Spanish church which has been spared this fate – kindled in the name of the Gospel – retains a disconcerting impression of a building tottering beneath a wealth of gold, jewels, and prominent monuments heaped in disorder below lofty altars and in innermost corners of the transepts.

Moissac: Cloister (after a nineteenth century engraving)

With the return to classicism, the wall of incomprehension which both cut short and preserved these witnesses of a Christianity, dead, probably, from excess and the universality of its own genius did not prevent there being an occasional case where the legacy was restored with touching fidelity. The most famous example of this occurred in the ancient city of Valence, seat of the diocese of the middle Rhône. In 1604 the municipality decided on an almost total reconstruction of the Romanesque cathedral which had been twice devastated in the religious wars, and stipulated that the builders should restore the pillars 'on the same foundations as the old ones, to the same shape, thickness and size as the ones still standing, and enriched with their original capitals.' The resulting building, dating from a period when the classical style was most popular, is a Romanesque pastiche able to deceive experts with its careful exactitude. The restorers even made use of surviving fragments, including two sculptured tympana which easily take their place amid the new work, lending it a little of their passionate feeling.

It is possible to find other examples of these outdated buildings being treated with a certain bold respect which may compensate for or excuse more brutal behavior. At Saint-Paulien, seat of a bishopric later transferred to Le Puy, the interior of the fine, large Romanesque church, threatened with ruin, was encased in a shell of masonry, medieval in conception, which preserved the original design intact with its wide, lofty cylindrical vault, the chevet prolonged by radial apses, and the exterior silhouette of the building marked by black and white incrustations.

These, however, are no more than happy exceptions. Most Romanesque buildings became gradually more removed from a society which repudiated them and, in the final period of the Ancien Régime, their glories gradually faded away. Nor was this situation peculiar to France.

8

Abbey of Cluny in 1157 (reconstruction after a drawing of
K. J. Conant).

Reports bear witness to the extent of the degrad-
ation and ruinous state of the buildings.
Revolutionary fanaticism and the stupidity of a
materialist society who used the stones from
these huge, useless hulks for the walls of ware-
houses and cottages, hastened their inevitable
downfall. The few examples of restoration are
outnumbered by the disasters recorded in
several districts of the new France. In Indre-et-
Loire, the basilica of Saint-Martin at Tours, one
of the most celebrated places of pilgrimage in
the country, was finally reduced to a ruin. In

Haute-Vienne, the abbey church of Saint-Martial at Limoges was demolished between 1792 and 1797. In Vienne, the extraordinary rotunda of the abbey church of Charroux was allowed to crumble irretrievably away. In the Côte-d'Or, a similar rotunda added by Abbot William to the east end of Saint-Bénigne at Dijon was also dismantled. Finally, in Saône-et-Loire, there was a zealous burning of the old church archives; fortified castles and large private houses were listed for demolition, and the huge abbey church of Cluny, without doubt the chief wonder of the Romanesque world, was systematically dismembered.

## An ambiguous resurrection

Following periods of revolution which disturb developing nations there frequently occur peculiar throwbacks. In France it was Chateaubriand's 'Génie du Christianisme' (1862) which provoked this startling revival of consciousness. The writer boldly set himself up 'within the ruined temples,' as he put it, to proclaim the values of faith, religion and prayer which the Revolution had planned to abolish from the hearts of the masses. The outstanding success of his book made it clear that the energy of the old fires had not yet cooled beneath the new formed ashes. The rehabilitation proclaimed by Chateaubriand extended to the arts as well. In an attack on the neo-classic architects of the time, he wrote: 'We build in vain elegant, well-lit Greek temples to house the congregations of the good people of Saint Louis. They will always regret the cathedral of Rheims and Notre-Dame de Paris, basilicas overgrown with moss and filled with generations of the dead and the souls of their forefathers . . . God is the everlasting law; his origins and everything pertaining to his worship should be lost in the darkness of time.' Due to such misconceptions – transformed by his superb prose – the Romantics were soon lost in admiration for the Middle Ages; a

Carcassonne: St Nazaire. Capital with foliage decoration.

Middle Ages from which they extracted not so much enlightenment as half-formed passions and the horrors of its religion. Chateaubriand set up the Gothic cathedral as the ideal embodiment of these daydreams, rediscovering in it the dim light of the sacred forests of antiquity.

While folk-tales and legends were being revived and romantically embroidered in England and Germany, Victor Hugo evoked in his novels a breathtaking vision of a vast cathedral, the symbol of this stirring passion. Countless engravings stirred the imagination with black silhouettes of storm-racked castles, hollow, ruined vaults, and arches outlined by sudden flashes of lightning against a cloudy sky. The churches which had to be built to replace these shattered naves, the ruined town and country houses, even the book illustrations, all appeared — disconcertingly — in the Gothic troubadour finery, which to our eyes seems laughable.

## Prosper Mérimée

One should not judge these vagaries too harshly. After several centuries of ostracism, the fiction which they maintain has resulted in legends which are still popular. Nevertheless, they conceal a far more solid core of reality – one that has been intuitively recognized by more enlightened scholars. After lying fallow for so long, the Romanesque world could only be rediscovered by oblique methods.

It was Prosper Mérimée who headed the revival. A complex, disconcerting character, well in advance of his contemporaries, he was born in 1803, a year after the publication of the 'Génie du Christianisme,' and died on September 23, 1870, three weeks after the battle of Sedan.

Few of his contemporaries knew him intimately, since he concealed himself beneath the mask of a sceptical dilettante, and treated his fellows with icy disdain. Only occasionally does a remark betray his loneliness and disillusion. We do not know the motives which prompted him to accept the post – offered him on account of his connexions – of Inspector General of the Monuments Historiques in 1833, succeeding an undistinguished writer, Vitet. He was only thirty and did not possess the slightest technical qualifications, but the new assignment undoubtedly brought out the best in him. He threw himself wholeheartedly into the work; and in his constant provincial tours in search of important medieval remains, in clear-sighted assessments of restoration work required and his subsequent supervision, he found an intellectual and spiritual satisfaction lacking in his social life. This is, moreover, clearly evident in his travel diaries.

## Viollet-le-Duc, theorist and prophet

Unlike the Romantics who turned to the Middle Ages to fulfil their own dreams, Mérimée thought of the buildings under his care as separate objective entities. By avoiding the sentimentality that had surrounded them, he revealed the genius of their construction. At the height of the Gothic Revival, he was one of the first (outside the narrow specialist circle of the commissioners of the Monuments Historiques) to understand and admire examples of Romanesque art as much as Gothic cathedrals. He supervized the restoration of Saint-Savin-sur-Gartempe and Vézelay, placing the latter in the hands of Eugène Viollet-le-Duc, then a still unknown architect aged twenty-six. The young man knew exactly how to tackle this risky task, and it is unrewarding now to comment on any of his eccentricities. Without him, Vézelay and many other buildings would no longer exist.

Less well-known is that the architect was also an exemplary and often prophetic theorist. In the preface to his monumental 'Dictionnaire raisonné de l'architecture,' written a century ago, he outlined a program which recent research has readopted as the sole key to medieval and, particularly, to Romanesque art. He grasped its scope, development and intricacies with amazing clarity as may be seen from the following passage:

'From the ninth to the fifteenth century the arts in France followed a regular, logical course, spreading outward to England, Germany, Northern Spain, Italy, Sicily and the East . . . Buildings of stone or wood perish . . . but the state of mind which has caused their erection is indestructible, and this state of mind is our own, the spirit of our country . . . It has seemed difficult to me to outline the successive transformation of the arts of architecture without simultaneously providing a sketch of the civilization for which this architecture provides an envelope. If this task turns out to be beyond my power, I shall have at least opened up a new method of approach . . . Putting

Vézelay: Abbey church. Interior view.

aside all sympathy for individual forms of art, I have been struck by the absolute harmony existing between the arts of the Middle Ages and the mental attitudes of the peoples among whom they developed . . . Maybe it is impossible to write a history of medieval architecture, as this means including and setting side by side the religious, political, feudal and social history of several nations. It is necessary to tabulate the various influences which resulted in the attainment of different standards in individual countries, to analyze their interaction and define the results; to take into account local traditions, tastes and customs, rules imposed by the use of materials, trade links, and the genius of individuals who influenced events either by hurrying them on or by causing them to turn aside from their natural courses. Finally, it is necessary to keep under observation the ceaseless investigations of a civilization in process of formation, and to immerse oneself in the religious and philosophic trends of the Middle Ages.'

Viollet-le-Duc also noted the twofold failure of research dependent either on classification of buildings by geographical factors, or on impersonal formal or stylistic grounds, or, as a last resort, based on blurred judgements steeped in the mystic symbolism common to the Romanesque world. Until quite recently Romanesque art was commonly regarded as no more than a preliminary to the rich perfection of Gothic, but now that it is clearly revealed as an end in itself, Viollet-le-Duc's suggestions, with their overtones of careful reserve, may be better understood. It has become obvious from more extended surveys that the field of Romanesque covers an almost infinite variety of types and aspects which just cannot be included in the traditional division into schools. The broad, elongated, unarticulated and unvaulted masses of eleventh century German churches have nothing in common with the clever articulation, vaulted elevations, and complex plans of St Sernin at

Speyer: Cathedral. General view (after a nineteenth century engraving).

is to offer additional proof that Viollet-le-Duc's method is the only one enabling a sufficiently extensive approach to the Romanesque world to be made.

## An ambiguous definition

However, there are stumbling blocks. Archeologists have long realized that the term Romanesque is both ambiguous and deceptive. Unlike the term Gothic, which has been in use for an additional three centuries, it carries no pejorative sense. The French adjective, 'roman,' was thought up as late as 1818 by an obscure scholar, Auguste Le Prévost, to express the analogy between the origins of the style and the formation of languages derived from Latin, thus known as romance tongues. Archeologists, steeped in the naturalist doctrine of evolution, were enthralled by the term for almost a century.

In English the root 'roman' became romanesque, in German 'roman-isch,' in Italian and Spanish 'roman-ico.' In England traces of the Romanesque are more extensive than is sometimes supposed, but the buildings are fewer and lack the originality of those of the early Gothic and curvilinear styles. In German lands, the authoritative imperial style and, later, the fantastic expansion of Gothic, for a long time concealed the intermediary architectural types dependent on the former and soon swept away by the latter which was more in keeping with the innermost spirit of these peoples. The architectural inventories of the Mediterranean countries are still far from complete. The survival of Early Christian architecture in Italy and the vigorous and lasting extension of both Byzantine and Moslem influences have – rather rashly – caused some archeologists to exclude almost the entire peninsular from the Romanesque domain. Spain (apart from Catalonia which has been surveyed by Puig i Cadafalch) has lagged behind

Toulouse and St Étienne at Nevers. The churches of Aquitaine with their rows of domes making for a series of independent interior spaces are completely different in style to the Cluniac buildings with their strong feeling of tension, their excessively high arches, narrow bays and ribbed vaults. The churches of Poitou with their exuberantly rich exteriors contrast with the disciplined layouts of the great abbey churches of Normandy. All attempts to create definitions based on constructional or decorative premises have ended in an impasse. Their chief advantage and is only now being thoroughly examined; all the more regrettable since the reconquered territories of Navarre and Castile, together with Portugal, contain some of the finest examples of Romanesque sculpture, and were clearly the favorite locations for late forms which served as models for Gothic arches and moldings.

Set boundaries must not be considered to cover exactly similar periods of time and technical developments in every country. Nor have the increasingly frequent discoveries of the early use of pointed arches in scattered parts of the Romanesque world served to curtail these discrepancies. The Italians, for instance, include in their schedule of Romanesque buildings some as late as the Broletto at Como which is after 1200, and the Palazzo dei Consoli at Gubbio, erected after 1300. German and young American architects tend to repudiate the categories favored by the French, preferring formal analyses which, all too often, are rather abstract and so weaken the strength of the historical background.

On the whole, revealing the extensive, contradictory influences which nourished the spirit of the Romanesque world is as commendable as the shadowy reconstruction of its inner growth and regional differences. Yet this is not enough. In fact, Romanesque artists, in their eagerness to gain knowledge, to transcribe and recreate, turned to every source – pagan antiquity, Byzantium, Syria and Armenia, and Ireland. They inherited a complete repertory compiled over seven centuries of Christianity. To reduce this to an amalgam or a simple synthesis leads to misunderstanding. The inner power of these sources of inspiration welded the inheritance of the past into a new force, impressing it, like potter's clay, with a new and vital impetus.

## Birth of the Romanesque world

This exciting achievement was produced in less than two centuries. Yet the dates defining the Romanesque styles which serve as basis for definitions, are often a source of argument. Archeologists agree that Romanesque art starts with the year 1000, founding this belief on one of the most famous passages in the whole of medieval literature: 'Shortly after the year 1000 it came about that churches were rebuilt practically throughout the world, and mainly in Italy and Gaul; and although most of them were very suitable, scarcely needing any alteration, all Christian peoples were seized with a great desire to outdo one another in magnificence. It was as if the world shook and cast off its old age, everywhere investing itself with the white mantle of churches.'

This vision of the monk, Raoul Glaber, a witness of the events he describes, has been the subject of innumerable expositions by historians and archeologists. It has also been the starting point of stories concerning the 'anguish' of the

Angers: St Martin. Example of a building c.1000.

14

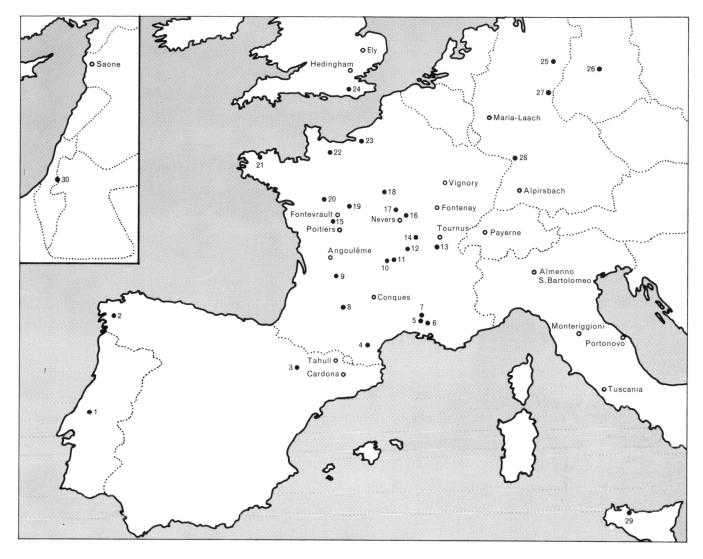

Map of the West showing principal places mentioned in the text.

| | | | |
|---|---|---|---|
| 1 Tomar | 9 Périgueux | 17 Charité-sur-Loire | 25 Hildesheim |
| 2 Santiago de Compostela | 10 Orcival | 18 Saint-Benoît-sur-Loire | 26 Merseburg |
| 3 Siresa | 11 Clermont | 19 Tours | 27 Hersfeld |
| 4 Carcassonne | 12 Châtel-Montagne | 20 Angers | 28 Speyer |
| 5 Saint-Giles-du-Gard | 13 Cluny | 21 St Pol-de-Léon | 29 Palermo |
| 6 Tarascon | 14 Paray-le-Monial | 22 Caen | 30 Jerusalem |
| 7 Uzès | 15 Saint-Généroux | 23 Jumièges | |
| 8 Moissac | 16 Vézelay | 24 Lewes | |

year 1000 which were so obligingly circulated by the Romantics. Modern scholarship has done justice to it, at the same time noting the aptitude of the medieval mind for condensing a complex sequence of events into a striking formula, transmuting them and instinctively interpreting the lesson to be learnt from them. All that Glaber did was to transcribe the slow social, economic, and political evolution centering around 1000 into an astonishingly abridged poetic image. It is not, however, inaccurate to date the Romanesque as beginning about the year 1000, but it is asking too much to maintain that its direct and immediate cause was sudden relief from the anguish of the millennium. This was neither as overwhelming nor as universal as has been sometimes made out.

# Plates

## Vignory, France: Church

21 General view of the nave. Carolingian basilican-type elevation with triforium. Each large arch at ground level is matched by two bays of the false triforium and one clerestory window. This makes for a calm rhythm completed by the triple bay of the west front.

22 The ambulatory with a tunnel vault supported on alternating pillars.

23 A twin bay of the triforium. The capital has a double head surmounted by a large block.

## Angoulême, France: Cathedral

24 Façade. This masterful composition is framed by two towers topped by modern pinnacles. It consists of five superimposed courses of arcades and round-headed windows held together by the great arch that envelops the center and a layer of lightly applied sculpture.

25 The tympanum of the central arch: Christ in majesty adored by two angels and surrounded by the symbols of the Evangelists.

26 The great pierced dome over the transept crossing.

27 One of the domes resting on pendentives over the nave.

## Fontevrault, France: Abbey kitchens

28 Exterior view of the Romanesque kitchens.

29 Detail, showing the octagonal pyramid of the main roof and the arrangement of the chimneys whose pinnacles add to the carefully thought out conceit of the silhouette.

30 The lofty central octagon with its supporting squinches.

31 Detail of the interior showing the skilful articulation of the plan and the supports backed by the masonry.

32 Two of the five surviving apses. The other three were destroyed in the sixteenth century. This is a good example of a link between religious and secular buildings: these alcoves could easily be mistaken for the apses of a church.

## Poitiers: Notre-Dame la Grande

33 The exterior from the chevet. The bell-tower rests on a great relieving arch and is surmounted by an elegant galleried lantern.

34 Façade, for comparison with that of Angoulême cathedral. Three rows of superimposed arcades are filled with the rich decorative sculpture favored in Aquitaine; this is always subject to a strictly controlled harmony.

35 The round-headed arches of the sanctuary.

36 Detail of the massive rounded pillars.

## Tournus: St Philibert

37 The two bell-towers from the chevet.

38 Upper portion of the nave. Slim stone columns with plain moldings, aisles with groined vaults, diaphragm arches making the bays of the center nave.

39 The nave from the upper storey of the narthex.

40 Detail of the nave with its transverse tunnel vault.

41 North walk of the cloister with its low groined vault.

42 Upper storey of the narthex. The lofty barrel vault supported on massive pillars is perfectly balanced by the quadrant-vaulted aisles.

43 Interior of the south tower of the narthex.

44 Chevet chapel with 'opus spicatum.'

**Vignory : Church**
Plan, analytical section and cross section 1 :400

0 1   5   10   15   M
0   10   20   50   FT

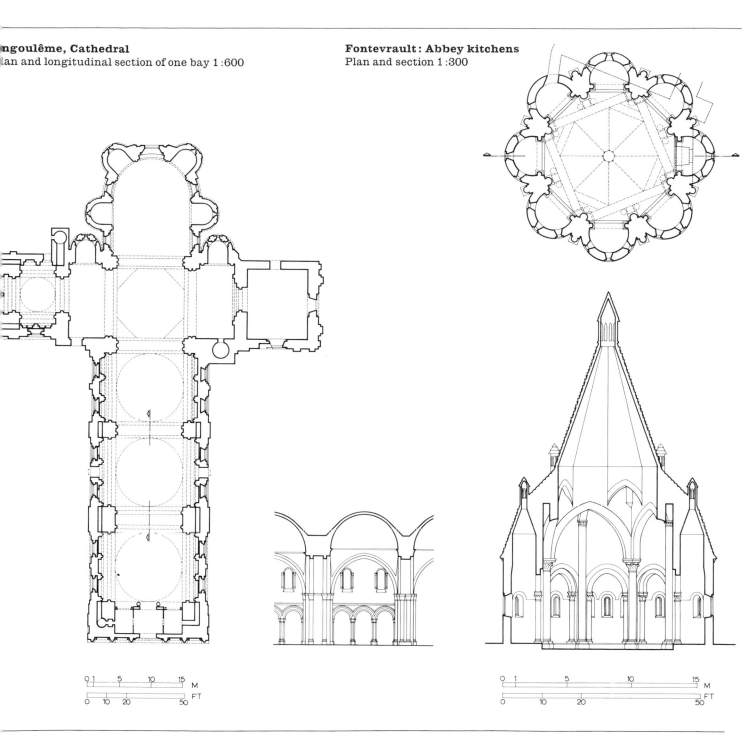

**ngoulême, Cathedral**
lan and longitudinal section of one bay 1:600

**Fontevrault: Abbey kitchens**
Plan and section 1:300

0 1 5 10 15 M
0 10 20 50 FT

0 1 5 10 15 M
0 10 20 50 FT

# Notes

## Vignory (France) : Church

This church in the diocese of Langres was given by Charlemagne to the monks of the Abbey of Luxeuil who seem to have lost it in a comparatively short space of time. About 1050, the local lord, Roger, presented it to the monks of the Abbey of St Bénigne at Dijon who established a priory there. The deed of gift specified that the church had been newly built and consecrated, but, in actual fact, as Deshoulières has established, the nave seems to have been constructed slightly later than the choir with its ambulatory and three radiating chapels. Two different architectural formulae may be found side by side in this fine, dignified building. The plan of the choir is of French origin and the unvaulted nave is in the Carolingian tradition. The latter receives its emphasis from the triforium which hollows out the nave walls with the same rhythm as the arches at ground level.

## Angoulême (France) : Cathedral

This magnificent building was over-restored in the nineteenth century by the architect Abadie, a fate shared by so many buildings surviving from the Middle Ages. It stands in the heart of Aquitaine, a vast district containing many churches roofed with a series of domes for which this was undoubtedly the prototype. The fact that the church was started by Bishop Girard de Blaye who had been a teacher of theology at Périgueux where he must have seen the commencement of the domes at St Etienne-de-la-Cité only serves to change the setting of one of the most difficult problems of Romanesque archeology. For we still do not know how this majestic, large-scale type of building with its strange hints of the East reached Périgueux. The cathedral of Angoulême has three circular domes over the nave, an octagonal dome with a drum lit from an arched gallery over the crossing, and a wide, semi-circular choir with four radiating chapels. The nave is fronted by a magnificent, lofty façade with traditional decorative wall arcades interpreted by the architect with especial fluency.

## Fontevrault (France) : Abbey kitchens

This is one of the most extraordinary buildings of Romanesque civil architecture. The Benedictine abbey of Fontevrault was founded by Robert d'Arbrissel, a friend of Girard de Blaye, and included a church, consecrated in 1119, vaulted with a series of domes in imitation of Angoulême cathedral. The abbey kitchens built a little earlier in the twelfth century, echo this constructional system. The plan is based on a square enclosed in an octagonal exterior punctuated by five small apses; this square is again split into a smaller octagon. A complex arrangement of pillars and arches supports the lofty, conical vault through which the smoke could escape by means of one main chimney and 17 secondary vents.

## Poitiers : Notre-Dame-la-Grande

Here there is an exciting contrast between the interior whose polychrome decoration does not affect the strict structural balance and the exterior silhouette with the high tiered belfry standing out behind the dazzling façade. In this case the lavish sculpture is contained in an architectural framework punctuated by three rows of superimposed arcades; above these is the undecorated area of the projecting pediment.

## Tournus : St Philibert

The abbey of Tournus, one of the oldest and most revered monastic foundations in Burgundy, was destroyed by Hungarian invaders in 937 and almost entirely reconstructed in the eleventh century. The building of the church was carried out by several successive workshops. The crypt, which may have determined the plan of the chevet of the upper church, is in the pre-Romanesque tradition with an ambulatory roofed by a tunnel vault which still bears marks of scaffolding. Lombard workmanship reigns supreme in the narthex which is a remarkable combination of tunnel, quadrant and groined vaults, its two successive storeys forming a solid structural core, bold and massive in effect. The lofty nave marks a further advance: it is roofed with daringly light transverse tunnel vaults and completed by a fine, skilfully designed choir.

22

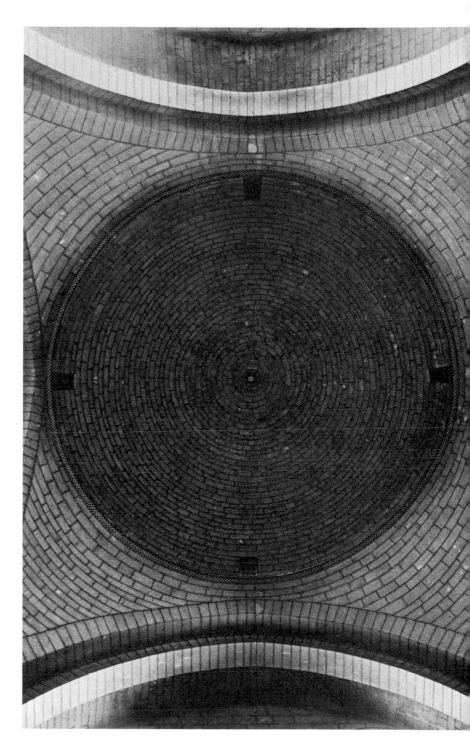

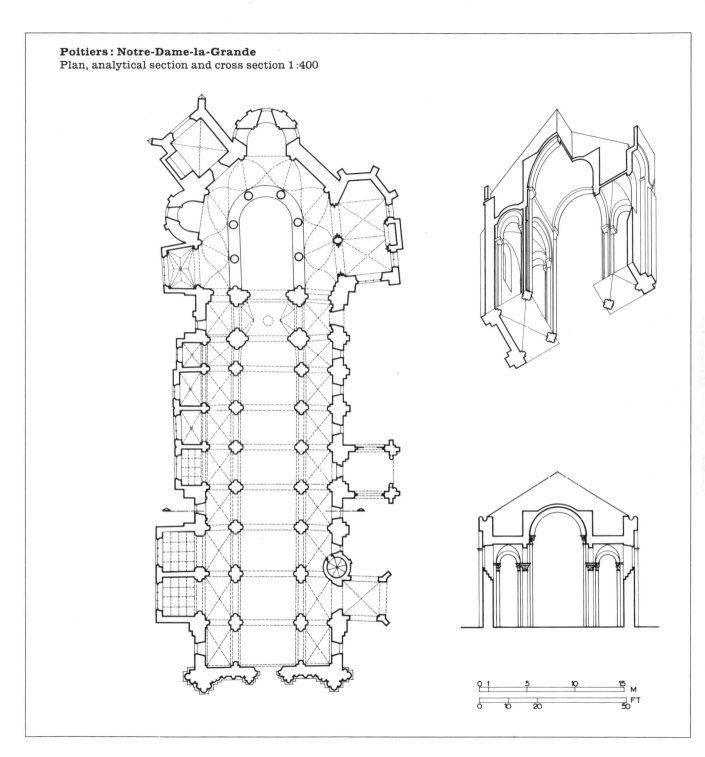

**Poitiers: Notre-Dame-la-Grande**
Plan, analytical section and cross section 1:400

0 1    5    10    15 M
0   10   20        50 FT

45

**Tournus : St Philibert**
Cross sections of narthex and nave, plan of crypt, general plan and longitudinal section 1:600

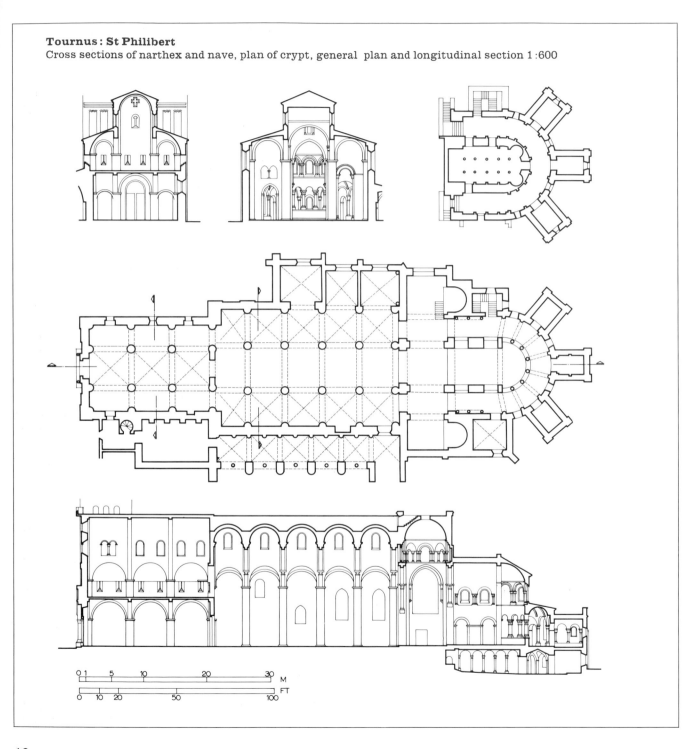

0 1  5  10  20  30  M
0 10 20  50  100 FT

# 1. Background to Romanesque

## From darkness to dawn. The last invasions of the tenth century

Glaber's account reflects a lull which goes far deeper than at first appears. The period of great invasions which had continually threatened the West for the past seven centuries had just come to a close, and religious building was about to reach perfection. Ever since the last years of Charlemagne's reign, Scandinavian pirates had periodically ravaged the coastal districts of the North Sea, the Channel, and the Atlantic. The most important regions of France – Aquitaine and Poitou, Touraine, the Loire valley, the Île-de-France, even Lower Burgundy, had all suffered irreparable damage throughout the course of the ninth century. In 911, however, Charles III found a way of holding these invincible hordes at bay, by concluding a treaty by which they were to be settled on the Lower Seine. From now on, according to Abbé Plat (whose findings have thrown an entirely new light on the birth of Romanesque art) the tenth century, though still troubled, became a great period for construction, especially in Touraine. Structures which had been burnt or demolished by the Normans were speedily rebuilt. An entirely new taste evolved, 'a point of departure towards a fresh, logical kind of art: using fine stone, decoration stemming from basic features, such as door-jambs, and color obtained not from inset bricks but from projecting string-courses opposing black and white and so bringing black walls to life. Apart from the solution to the problem of vaulting, all the ingredients of the later Romanesque style were already apparent in these buildings.'

Scarcely was the danger halted on this side than it was renewed from the east. During the early tenth century, Magyar horsemen invaded German and Lombard territories. In 913 they reached the frontiers of Burgundy, and, in 924, scoured the Rhône valley. They were severely defeated by Emperor Otto I in 937, but re-attacked

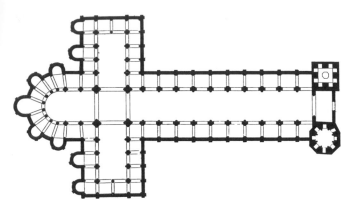
Tours : St Martin. Reconstructed plan (with later belfry).

Burgundy. It was not until 955 that Otto finally overpowered them at Lechfeld before Augsburg. The Hungarians then gradually settled in the Danube plain and the ensuing conversion of Stephen, their king, (997-1038) sealed the peace. This was followed by an artistic and intellectual revival instigated by the Emperor and his sons. As we shall see, architecture played a vital part in this, distinguished by the continuance of Early Christian and Carolingian formulae. Some of the noteworthy innovations of this period, including the siting of a transept organically linked to the other limbs of the building, lead directly to the cruciform Romanesque plan, the basic core of its finest developments.

In the South, Saracen pirates added to the devastation. The victory won by Charles Martel over the Saracens near Poitiers in 732 probably halted the invaders, but did not end the insecurity which was long felt in the South. The forces of Islam gained a hold in Spain where, from time to time, they made dangerous penetrations northwards, leaving the Christian princes of the Asturias with no more than some precarious fortresses in the coastal mountains. In 997, Almanzor destroyed the national shrine of Santiago de Compostela. After Spain the Saracens had no difficulty in conquering the islands of the Mediterranean. They occupied Sicily in 827 and in 846 followed the course of the Tiber to the gates of Rome. Subsequently they gained a footing in Corsica, Sardinia, and Calabria and, at the end of the century, established a firm bridgehead in the Provençal massif of Le Freinet which dominates the Gulf of Saint-Tropez and guards the way to the hinterland. Having dug themselves in, they increased their raids on Provence and the Rhône valley and infiltrated deep into the valleys of the Alps. In 906 they laid waste the great abbey of Novalesa at the foot of the Mont-Cenis, penetrated the Maurienne, Tarantaise, and the Valais, and reached as far as the Grisons. The extent of these disasters is indicated by the breaks in the episcopal lists in most of the southern and Lower Alps dioceses. There was complete suspension of all administrative life and the ancient, fertile province was frighteningly silent. The diocese of Grenoble was deserted and had to be repopulated. Traffic over the Alps was harassed by well disciplined, rival bands. About 940 one of these bands attacked and destroyed the monastery of Agaune, and in 972 another captured Saint Mayeul, Abbot of Cluny, only releasing him on payment of a large ransom. This last incident led to the final counter-attack : William, Count of Provence, and his brother, Robert, led the Christians in a successful assault on Le Freinet.

The coastal regions of Provence were to be threatened by the barbarian for a long time, and life there was slow to revive. Romanesque progress was consequently also slow and its chief masterpieces at Arles and Saint-Gilles are more or less contemporary with Notre-Dame in Paris. Unlike Christian Spain, Provence gained nothing from the Moslems. Nevertheless, the events of 972 were universally significant. Thanks to them the routes across the Alps were now finally freed and the way was reopened for exchanges between Italy, France and the German lands. There is a definite connexion between the easing of this situation and the migrations of craftsmen from Como who, with an extraordinary aptitude for expansion, conveyed their obscurely elaborated building techniques through the valleys and over the Alpine passes to distant countries.

## The turning point of 1140.
## Suger and the light of the Gothic

Romanesque art became absorbed in the emerging style of Gothic before becoming decadent, and gave a repertory of proved techniques, a whole battery of new architectural inventions, and an iconography whose main themes were to remain fixed for several centuries. The date, method, and character of this achievement varied, however, from one district to another. The Gothic style appeared early in the Île-de-France, but did not reach the Lyonnais or the southern provinces until the late twelfth century, while Central Europe had to wait until the thirteenth century. Western France, for long

Diagonal rib vault.

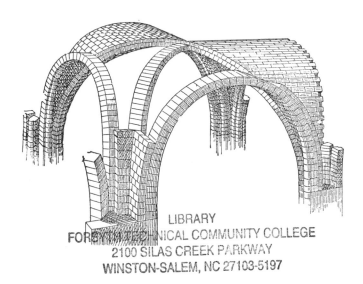

highly individual, and Languedoc, struck by the severe after-effects of heresy, adopted forms that were basically different to the graceful nobility of Noyon and Chartres. The developments of English Gothic continued independent of the Continental styles; in less than two centuries it reached a point which was not attained elsewhere for four hundred years.

The current theory is that the appearance of the new style was marked by the use of the rib vault. Certainly its adoption gradually brought about basic modifications in the interior and exterior arrangement of buildings. Yet in England, Lombardy, and South-West France, use had already been made of rib vaults, at any rate in experimental guise, to reinforce groined vaults. There was no immediate and overwhelming change in the outlines or interior arrangements of the great churches either in the center of France or on its boundaries. The plan of the cathedral at Langres, for instance, which was building from 1141 to 1196, remains typically Romanesque of the School of Cluny. We have to wait until the 1180's for the invention of the flying buttress, which put an end to the sad sight of bulging arches and made possible the wide, lofty perforations, so notable a feature of the new style. All the same, this association of two technical contrivances is not enough to define a system. In actual fact, a deep spiritual and intellectual gap separates the styles of the Romanesque from the budding style of Gothic, maintaining and, in retrospect, restoring, the sovereign independence of the former. The abbey church of Saint-Denis is a far better expression and symbol of the Gothic genius than a catalogue of constructional progress. It represents the unique, subjective vision of Abbot Suger: he did not conceive it as a purely functional assemblage of stones and stresses, but as the expression and support of his own metaphysical beliefs. That he was able to do this was due to earlier craftsmen's achieve-

49

ments which he inherited and used.

## The Council of Sens, outlet of the mystique of the Romanesque

1140 was a vitally important year: in its course, both Peter Abelard's work was condemned and Abbot Suger's venture at Saint-Denis was begun. It has too often been stated that the Council of Sens was a triumph of conservative monks, hostile to all intellectual progress, over the prophetic theology of Abelard. It would be more accurate to say that it was a conflict between two incompatible theological conceptions, and now it is vain to suggest that one is inferior to the other.

The processes of Suger's thought were enclosed in this program. A superb artist, his sole inspiration lay in the static beauty of God's house. In its contemplation he could not rest until he had actively associated it with his own thought so that, through it, he could see himself 'residing, as in reality, in some strange region of the universe which does not wholly exist either in the filth of the earth or in the purity of the heavens.' While theologians were busy plumbing the unfathomable mystery of transubstantiation, and alchemists, to a lesser degree, made desperate attempts to turn matter to gold, Suger boldly broke up natural daylight, transmuting it by means of 'the charm of multi-colored gems' which he set in the reduced thickness of the stone. This new form of 'wonderful and uninterrupted' light which spread over his church was not only meant to beguile the eye; its purpose was also to uplift the mind and soul.

Such philosophical themes were probably not completely new. There is a great distance, however, between abstract theory and Suger's own stupendous creation, the building of which is held to be his by right. Its revolutionary construction is as important, in its own way, as

St Pol-de-Léon (Finistère): Church. Main nave (after a modern architectural drawing).

the sudden intrusion of concrete into modern building methods. Throughout its many regional variations Romanesque architecture extracted its power from a twofold effect common to all of them: the dynamic power of cleverly adjusted masses held by faultless articulation, and the movement of interior walls, sometimes stressed and sometimes opposed by polychrome decoration. These were the qualities which made up its individual genius. The Gothic cathedral, on the other hand, which rose out of Suger's dream

50

world, fulfilled itself as an atmospheric envelope, an ever-changing halo caressing the inert bone structure. Structually, the cathedrals of Chartres and Léon are identical, though they blaze with opposed stresses reflecting historical and temperamental differences. In general, however, they are pure light.

It was the individual technique of stained glass which effected this subtle transformation. This, combined with the rib vault sustaining the ever sharper tension of the interior, and the flying buttress allowing the reduction of the stone skeleton to a simple reticulation, was the sole factor in the realization of mature Gothic, and the efforts of three centuries concentrated on these glowing features. Simultaneously, Abbot Suger (friend of Peter the Venerable who did not go beyond completing the Romanesque work of St Hugh at Cluny and of St Bernard who refused to countenance appeals to the senses in his Cistercian churches) signed the death warrant of the principles of Romanesque in the very act of crowning them. By this total, conscious engagement of his spiritual and intellectual personality, he somehow bent to his own use and dismembered the mysterious balance between man's creative desire and the interplay of living stone.

## A slow but irresistible transfer

There is no stopping the march of history, though similarities may be seen in retrospect. It was no pure chance that Suger, creator of the French cathedral type that was gradually to spread over the whole of Europe, was also the friend and most influential advizor to the king of France — and the king's regent during his absence at the Crusades. The two centuries of the Romanesque had gradually prepared the way for his undoubted primacy by shifting the center of gravity of the Christian world. Henceforward there was to be no return to the momentarily imagined ideal of the City of God manifested on earth.

In 962, Otto I, then at the height of his political power, followed the example of Charlemagne and received the imperial crown from the hands of the Pope in Rome. The purpose of this act was not only to set a seal on the agreement emphasizing that the Papacy was dependent on the Empire. The Emperor was claiming the foundation of a stable order based on the Christian faith, and he well knew that no one in the West would contest this privilege with him. To the German Emperor all dreams of a hegemony seemed permissible, and architecture was the foremost of the arts to bear witness to the imperial splendor.

Just as Charlemagne had done before him, Otto turned to Byzantium, marrying his son to the daughter of Emperor John Tzimisces. Under his grandson, Otto III, the Empire was enriched by an ascendancy which benefited the whole of Europe. Between the Emperor, known to posterity by the strange and untranslatable title of 'mirabilia mundi,' and Gerbert of Aurillac, who became Pope Sylvester II in 999, there existed a bond of souls. This was the majesty of the Pax Romana without recourse to arms and, in a deeper sense, the humble discovery and penitential atonement for the sin which every man bears within himself. Otto died prematurely in 1002, and his death marked a fault in the political development of Europe. Before the end of the century his utopian coalition was to be brutally shattered against the rock of Canossa.

The entire situation changed. In the eleventh century the Papacy was no longer weak and docile as it had been in the previous century. Hildebrand succeeded to the throne of St Peter, as Gregory VII, in 1073. Born a Tuscan peasant he had taken his vows in the Benedictine monastery of St Mary on the Aventine, became chaplain to Pope Gregory VI and then a monk at Cluny where he had contact with Abbot Odilo and Grand Prior Hugh. Subsequently he was made a cardinal, became advizor to Leo IX, and legate in France and Germany. By his fearless attitude he roused the anger of the German king, Henry IV, who coldly deposed him at Worms with the aid of a council loyal to his interests. Gregory's reply was to absolve Henry's German subjects from all obligations to their sovereign. Their stern reconciliation at Canossa was only temporary and the return to antagonism lasted until the hard won Concordat of Worms in 1122.

## Cluny, motive force of Romanesque civilization

The dramatic repercussions of this antagonism were confined to the two protagonists – Germany vacillating between the Pope and the Emperor, and papal Italy. The whole of Europe, however, suffered from this surge of trouble. Apart from equivocal supporters and secret opportunists the Holy See at least had the ever loyal support of the strength of Cluny brought to its zenith by a century and a half of progress. By the express desire of its founder, Duke William of Aquitaine, the small community on the banks of the Grosne was recognized as a direct possession of St Peter under whose patronage the Duke had purposely placed it. It continued to be granted exemption

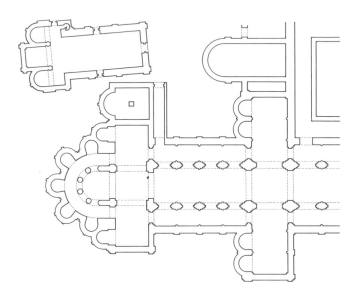

Lewes, England: Priory. Plan of the eastern section of the church revealed by excavations. It is almost a replica of the abbey church of Cluny.

by the Popes with the result that its expansion was based on a jealously maintained independence of the local temporal and spiritual powers which, throughout the tenth century, were both enfeebled and of mutual assistance to one another. Already, however, the eminent Abbots of Cluny, Odo, Aimard, and Mayeul, were transforming their humble monastery into a powerful influence and initiating a much needed reform of the Church and its morals. Bound by affection and a mutual deference to the rulers of Germany, Mayeul and his successor, St Odilo of Mercoeur, acclaimed their consecration as Emperors, and Hugh of Semur who followed Odilo in 1049 was Henry IV's sponsor. The subsequent struggle between the German king and Gregory VII put him in an embarrassing and uncomfortable position. At Canossa he wholeheartedly interceded for the penitent king, but he was, and continued to be, on the Pope's side. When, a few years later, Gregory, in order to repay the Abbot for his loyalty, publicly praised the abbey of

Cluny: Abbey church of SS Peter and Paul. Plan.

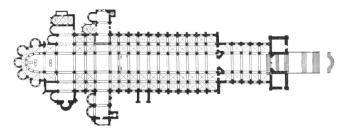

Cluny he was only reaffirming what was well known already. Though formerly uninfluential, the protection of the reaffirmed papacy was a powerful aid to the consolidation of the vigour of Cluny which simultaneously made a return offering of its prestige and vast resources. The

St Gilles-du-Gard: Church. Portal.

Popes strengthened the abbey with privileges and guarantees extending to the entire Congregation together with its priories overseas.

Gregory VII never renounced his role of Cluniac monk even when he succeeded as supreme head of the Church, and Popes Urban II and Pascal II who followed him were also Cluniacs. Pope Gelasius II who had been forcibly expelled from Rome by Henry IV came to die at Cluny in 1119, and his successor, Calixtus I, was elected there.

When, after the death of Honorius II, the Pierleoni faction set up the antipope Anacletus II in opposition to the newly elected Innocent II, Abbot Peter the Venerable, unlike the vacillating Bernard of Clairvaux, immediately declared for Innocent, received him and give him encouragement. It is no exaggeration that, from 1049 until the end of the schism in 1138, the fortunes of the Roman church could be identified with those of Cluny.

## An apogee of building history

The Romanesque reached its zenith in the century hinging on the year 1095 when Urban II proclaimed the Crusade, and it would be pointless to ask what this civilization would have been without Cluny. However, we should recall that, besides the great abbey church built by St Hugh, many of its outstanding masterpieces were also Cluniac properties or foundations. In Burgundy the list includes Vézelay rebuilt by Renaud of Semur, the grand-nephew of St Hugh, Paray-le-Monial, and St-Germain at Auxerre; in French-speaking Switzerland, Payerne and Romainmôtier; in Nivernais, St Etienne at Nevers, La-Charité-sur-Loire, and Saint-Révérien; in Bourbonnais, Souvigny, and Châtel-Montagne; in Provence, Saint-Marcel-les-Sauzet, and Ganagobie; in Roussillon, Arles-sur-Tech; in Languedoc, Saint-

Gilles-du-Gard, Morlaas, Moissac, Figéac, Marcilhac, Carennac, and Beaulieu; in Auvergne, Saint-Géraud at Aurillac, and Mozat; in Limousin, Saint-Martial, Chambon, La Souterraine, and Uzerche; in Saintonge, Saint-Eutrope; in Poitou, Montierneuf; in the Île-de-France, Longpont, and Saint-Leu-d'Esserent; in England, Lewes; in Spain, Frómista. These names are chosen at random from among the astonishing list of Cluniac buildings surveyed by Dr Joan Evans. Above all they bear witness to the eclecticism of Cluny which never imposed itself as a prototype on any of its daughter foundations and, despite the organic centralization favored by Abbots Odilo and Hugh, allowed individual regional tastes free development.

## The trend towards a new asceticism

This flexible independence did not survive the decline of the Cluniacs. With the early years of the twelfth century the Cistercians and, to a lesser extent, the Cartusians took up the position formerly held by Cluny in religious affairs. The original asceticism of the Carthusians, the austerity enjoined on the Cistercians by St Bernard, and the evolution of history

Cistercian abbey of Sénanque. Cloister, an example of Cistercian architecture.

itself, now determined the prototypes to which builders throughout Christendom had to refer. The creation of the military orders also reinforced this ascetic approach to religion. The conventual churches of the Templars and Hospitalers were not outstanding for their size or fine architecture, most of them being plain, small-scale buildings. This aspiration to poverty, a reaction against the excessive luxury of the Church, even extended to Peter the Venerable, despite his artistic heritage. Very significantly it also agrees with the opinions expressed by Peter Abelard in the directives which he wrote to Héloise. In fact, it was the aspiration of all the monastic reformers of the late eleventh century and, moreover, coincided with the movement in Islam which just as firmly repudiated the rich decorations and facings of the mosques of Spain and the Maghreb. Thus it is not out of place at this point to draw attention to the fact that one of the earliest examples of this change in architectural style is to be found in Aragon, a region which had contacts with both Christian and Moslem civilization. In the late eleventh century the royal Augustinian foundation of Siresa hidden in one of the valleys of the Pyrenees chose a completely austere approach which was strictly opposed to all ornamental or figurative experiments.

## The emergence of Capetian France

The brutal break between the German Empire and the Holy See was not the whole background to the rise, triumph and decline of the Romanesque. This cycle also included the slow but sure advance of a political fortune which could not have been predicted in 1000. The royal house of Capet rose from humble origins in 987 and was accorded a rather condescending protection by the German Emperor. Very soon, however, various bold acts of intervention revealed the scope of its designs for the future. When Hugh Capet summoned Mayeul, Abbot of Cluny, to reform his abbey of Saint-Denis, his primary aim was probably the well-being of souls and the monks, but there was also a secondary motive; the alliance which he offered meant that from henceforward he was a power to be reckoned with. Despite feudal resistance, the young dynasty continued to exert its authority throughout the eleventh and twelfth centuries. It enlarged its territories at every opportunity and established and strengthened its prestige by a series of arbitrations and conquests which embraced the distant states of Burgundy and Auvergne.

## Youth of the Romanesque world

The slow movement of the scales of fate with its tragic reversals resulted in there being a completely different balance of power in the West to that which existed at the time of Otto I's coronation in 962, though it must be agreed that Romanesque architecture only partly reflected the change. Against this backcloth of political evolution a still more basic act was being played out in strict anonymity. The chief sign of this was probably a demographic progress which was not really discerned until quite recently, but the facts are now starting to emerge, thanks to the latest research. The widespread needs of the 1050's resulted in the greatest increase in the world's cultivated surface since prehistoric times and it is not too much to say that the basic features of the landscape of Western Europe were established at this period.

Recent research has tended to reject the traditional theory that the dioceses of the Church were strictly based on the administrative divisions of Roman cities; instead, a much later religious organization has been suggested, possibly parallel with the Carolingian civil divisions and finally completed by a series of frontier arrangements and internal groupings. If this view is adopted, Romanesque civilization did not develop in a world which had long been static, but in the midst of complex changes and a lively chain of evolution. Throughout the eleventh and twelfth centuries, rival religious houses continued to be constituted, and abbey charters other than those of Cluny bear witness to the foundation of country priories devoted to cultivation of the land. The great trade routes were reopened with a lively increase in traffic across the Alps now freed from local raiders; merchants from Flanders, the Rhineland, and the cities of Lombardy mingled with soldiers in the field, abbots on their missions, and pilgrims on their way to Rome. Suburbs with shops sprang up around abbeys sited near city gates, and an invigorating taste for adventure succeeded the heavy social inertia of the tenth century. Undoubtedly one of the most striking expressions of this mood was the development of pilgrimages.

In fact, these had never completely ceased. Even during the most troubled years of the ninth and tenth centuries, bold spirits kindled with enthusiasm and braved every kind of danger to embrace the rock of Calvary and kiss the tombs of the apostles. With the eleventh century, however, began a troubled period which once more disproved the theory of a new dawn about to break. The mad Caliph, Hakim, sacked and destroyed the Latin foundations and, afterwards, the Byzantine Emperors took the place of those of the West in the task of restoring and safeguarding the Holy Places. Roman Christendom, however, was tortured by remorse and filled with desire to regain the tomb of Christ even more than the pilgrimage road which had never been completely cut even at the period of the worst setbacks. When the Cluniac Pope, Urban II, proclaimed the Crusade at Clermont-Ferrand, he roused an indescribable enthusiasm which showed that the time was ripe. The results of his expedition, the conquest of Palestine and the establishment of the Latin kingdom were manifold. In the field of architecture, the building of the Romanesque Church of the Holy Sepulcher was an outward sign both of the power and love of the Crusaders. The principle of the orientation of churches was so strongly ingrained in this generation sated with symbolism that, even in the hard-won city of Jerusalem, the new shrine had its chevet at the east end like any other church. To Constantine's rotunda which had last been reconstructed to the orders of Emperor Constantine Monomachos in 1045 was added a compact, cruciform design with a wide projecting transept and a semi-circular choir surrounded by an ambulatory with three radiating chapels. On the south is a double entrance door between the belfry on the left and the square Calvary Chapel on the right. The building was consecrated in 1149 and offers a combination of styles inherited from East and West, including motifs from Poitou, Burgundy and Languedoc. There is even a rib vault over the transepts.

This impressive building dominated a vast

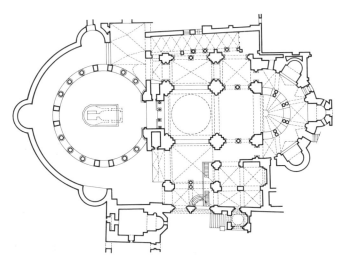

Jerusalem: Church of the Holy Sepulcher. Plan.

development program of churches, monasteries, commanderies, and hospices balancing the securing of the frontier defences by the huge fortresses of Beaufort, Margat, and Krak des Chevaliers. These cyclopean buildings with their formidable roughstone walls covered with mason's marks and their moats hollowed out of the rock are, in fact, the forerunners of modern casemates and concrete shelters and emanate the same feeling of stifling oppression. This large-scale undertaking introduced western building methods to the East while, simultaneously, the sight of the fabulous treasures of Byzantium kindled fresh flames in the ever lively imaginations of Christian builders.

The continually renewed vitality of this generation ensured that the drift to the Crusades had little or no effect on the strength of their native lands. The Crusades, however, far from impeding the progress of building in the West, enriched it with new found discoveries. By focusing the attention of rough and violent people on a single ideal, they gave an outlet to turbulent spirits without injuring their native lands.

The same overflow of abundant energy, at a somewhat more realistic level, brought about the twofold conquest of England and Southern Italy by the Normans less than two hundred years after their establishment in 911. They introduced their great timber-roofed churches with hollow walls and lantern towers to Britain and, between 1066 and 1189, built no fewer than twelve hundred castles which gradually benefited from lessons learned by military architects in the preparations of the defences of the Holy Land; the ruins of many of these may be seen today throughout England and Wales. In their Mediterranean territories, at Monreale, Palermo, and Cefalù, they produced the most amazing blends of Arab, Byzantine, and Nordic influences to be found in the Romanesque world.

The two other major pilgrimages to Rome and Santiago de Compostela were somewhat less dangerous than that to the Holy Land and, from the tenth to the twelfth century, were almost equally popular. The restoration work on the route undertaken by King Alfonso V in the early years of the eleventh century coincided with the progress of the spread of the Gospel among the Basques who soon freed the western passes of the Pyrenees. The stubborn forcing back of the Arabs crowned by the conquest of the Rioja enabled Alfonso VI of Castille to pursue the systematic organization of the fine road which soon received the title of 'camino.' This great work involved the building of several bridges and showed that, contrary to what has often been supposed, the Romanesque genius did not scorn material aids to achieve versatility. The power of Cluny came to the aid of the undertaking, made itself felt throughout the road's dangerous length, and effectively lent its support. The movement of countless pilgrims across the lands of Christendom, ships going to and fro across the sea beneath the equivocal sign of the Cross, treasures scattered, like the gifts of the Magi, round the slabs on which rest the witnesses of Christ, hymns and songs enfolding the marchers — all this ferment lies at the very heart of Romanesque civilization.

The renown and fame of the three great pilgrimages should not conceal the passion which urged other crowds towards minor pilgrimages. From East to West, countless litanies forged a chain which was soon to arm the whole of Christendom. The assurance reflected by the Romanesque world in the midst of disorder, paraphrased in its epics and revealed by the imprint of its buildings on the earth, was primarily due to the realization of racial pride.

## The theory of 'schools'

From this angle, Romanesque civilization seems to consist of more than a fortunate conjunction of economic pressures and a number of scattered roads in the West reopened after the continued disturbances of seven centuries. Its vast scope, the range of its discoveries, and its strange contrasts have puzzled archeologists and art historians. The theory of 'provincial schools' formulated by the chief French archeologists of the nineteenth century carries little weight today.

To start with, insufficient knowledge concerning Spain, Italy, Germany, Eastern and Central Europe, restricted such classification to France itself. This was, in fact, a refutation of the profound idea of Christianity which fermented the spiritual life of the Romanesque in the eleventh and twelfth centuries transcending specific regional differences. Just as serious was the erection of barriers between architectural expression in France and in other countries whose inventiveness was revealed by later research. Further harm also resulted from the forging of false links, too often the result of narrow-minded prejudice, as in the case of Spanish Romanesque art (a problem sufficiently complex in itself).

With regard to France, the theory of schools will probably be found accurate in trial investigations and will at least offer a convenient framework for more detailed research. It suggests a relationship between building styles and the territories where they have sunk their roots. Using it to conjure up the churches of Normandy, Poitou, Saintonge, Angoumois, the Bordelais, Languedoc, Auvergne, Provence, Burgundy, and the districts bordering the Rhine does more than merely supply the architectural map of France with a brilliant parade of buildings. It also serves to brush up each section of a harmoniously composed picture which satisfies both reason and the seeing eye by excluding the irrational and the disturbing influence of the unexpected.

This form of classification shares the draw-backs common to all forms of systematization. Its terminology is, historically, anachronistic, as it is based on a partition of the kingdom into provinces which did not, in fact, occur until later and then included important divisions such as Bourbonnais, Berry, and Maine which are almost passed over in the classification. All archeologists have admitted that the boundaries of the schools do not inevitably coincide with these political divisions, but, even so, the nominal agreement is, more often than not, shown to be arbitrary and too rigidly fixed. Within one of these schools may be found several parallel types which force one to create minor groups so that this authoritative theory is finally dispersed in a multitude of exceptions.

This doctrine of schools has recently been under fire from the younger generation of arche-ologists, including Pierre Lavedan, who after reaffirming the extraordinary splitting up of territory, comes to the direct conclusion that the method is a bad one. Instead, he proposes an entirely new definition based on the vaulting system adopted in the main nave. He disting-uishes three groups: churches with tunnel or groined vaults without galleries over the aisles; churches with tunnel or groined vaults with galleries over the aisles; and, finally, churches vaulted with a series of domes. The first category includes Burgundy which is split into three architectural divisions, Poitou and Provence; the second comprises the fine series of churches in the region of Clermont-Ferrand and the group known as churches of the pilgrimage roads; and the third besides the compact group of domed churches in Angoumois, Périgord and Quercy, three separate buildings which seem to have little connexion with one another or their surroundings: St Hilaire at Poitiers, Solignac, and the cathedral at Le Puy.

This classification at least has the advantage of being original. Cleverly avoiding previous theories, it acknowledges the basic preoccupa-tion of the Romanesque builders – the search for a vaulting system which maintained an even balance, and takes note of the varied solutions proposed. From time to time, churches of timber construction were destroyed by great fires and this encouraged their builders to use stone instead of inflammable materials. Stone vaults also lent an interior far greater dignity, unity and structural solidity than could be obtained from timber vaults or flat ceilings. To limit the field of Romanesque expansion to vaulted churches is, however, too severe a restriction and involves the entire elimination of Scandin-avia. The timber-roofed naves of the eleventh and twelfth centuries do not indicate the survi-val of an outdated tradition in church building; they pursue and develop individual construc-tional experiments in the fields of rhythmic elevation and the division of masses which are no less revolutionary than the vaults devized by Romanesque architects.

## Communication

From this point of view, it is not surprising that Pierre Lavedan's bold suggestion has failed to be universally accepted by archeologists. Some, like Henri Focillon, have turned aside from the controversial question of schools and devoted themselves to formal and stylistic analysis. Others, including Joseph Gantner, have extoled the intense spiritual feeling of an art in which God speaks and reigns supreme over any form of technical apparatus, while others again modest-ly prefer to salvage and adopt those portions of the theory of schools which still have validity. They oppose the factor of interregional com-munication brought about by roads to the sealed divisions of purely local dissemination.

There was a precedent for this theory. Gaston

Paris had already recognized the 'chansons de geste' as descended from the popular songs based on vague memories of history which strolling players spread abroad along the highways. Joseph Bédier, however, considered that he could prove that the pilgrimage roads had influenced the elaboration and diffusion of these epic legends. These viewpoints had the joint result of diminishing the individual authority of a single gifted poet, replacing it with the gradual emergence of an anonymous tradition. Bédier's thesis was enthusiastically received by some and bitterly criticized by others. The 'Song of Roland,' the most famous of the long poems, provided a focal point for this dispute, each side producing their fair share of valid arguments. The traditionalists left no stone unturned while their adversaries claimed that such a homogeneous masterpiece could only be the work of a single inspired poet. In all probability the truth lies midway between these two extremes.

## The 'churches of the pilgrimage roads'

This argument can also be used to throw fresh light on Romanesque archeology, in which sphere it is equally applicable. Bédier's theory was sufficiently alluring for attempts to be made to extend it to the buildings distributed along the four great routes across France starting from the major shrines of Tours, Vézelay, Le Puy and St Gilles whence, in accordance with the 'Pilgrims' Guide to Santiago,' they led the worshippers of the saint to his tomb in Galicia. The school known as that of 'the pilgrimage roads' includes only three surviving buildings: the abbey church of Conques, the church of St Sernin at Toulouse, and the cathedral of Compostela. There were also, however, two churches now destroyed: the pilgrimage shrine of St Martin at Tours and the abbey church of St Martial at Limoges. The building of these five churches extended over the whole of the eleventh century and carried on into the next, maintaining remarkable fidelity to the original conception. This was on a generous scale to allow for the handling of large crowds; chevets were prominently developed and allowance was made for movement around the high altar; both transepts and naves were flanked by aisles, and above these were quadrant vaulted galleries with twin arches opening on to the nave. The spread of this formula resulted in some striking buildings elsewhere including St Remy at Rheims, Saint-Sauveur at Figéac, and churches at Marcilhac and St Gaudens. Connexions may also be noted with the great Romanesque churches of Lower Auvergne, and the harmonious ternary rhythm of St Étienne at Nevers plainly seems to derive from it.

These discoveries have also been applied to other pilgrimage roads. Jean Vallery-Radot examined the routes of St Michael leading from Mont-St-Michel by way of St Michel d'Aiguilhe in Velay and the Sacra di San Michele in Piedmont to the Gargano and has shown that they conveyed certain architectural affinities, while more recently, George Nebolsine has surveyed those leading to Rome over the Alpine passes of the district of Como. The American archeologist, Kingsley Porter, caused a stir with his discovery of the sculpture of the pilgrimage roads and Jean Hubert, by means of a cartographic survey, aimed to establish that masterpieces of monumental sculpture in France were connected with the great road established by the Cluniacs between France and Santiago.

## Churches with series of domes

There also arose a simultaneous belief that it was possible to solve another riddle of Romanesque architecture which had formed a stumbling block in the classification of provincial schools, by recourse to the theory of roads. Aquitaine possesses a magnificent group of churches spread out across Angoumois, Saintonge, Périgord, Quercy and the Limousin, which are vaulted with a series of domes. These roof choir, nave and transepts, as well as the crossing. This arrangement results in a startling monumental effect completely different to the narrow divisions formed by the more usual vaulted naves: it expands the interior space to the greatest possible extent and the resulting plan is defined by a succession of perfect squares penetrated by waves of light and providing total visibility as there are no interior pillars. There is a rhythmic sense of movement from bay to bay which seems to be inspired by the swelling domes. The outer areas are only fully developed in the chevets with their small radiating apses. In periods of insecurity such as the crusade against the Albigensians and the Hundred Years' War, these buildings were easily adaptable for defence purposes.

There is no doubt that this type of church is of Eastern or Byzantine origin, but their grouping and distribution remain subjects of discussion. Geological reasons have been brought forward, including the chalky limestone of Aquitaine, a flexible substance easily hewn into the most difficult shapes. Nevertheless, there are other equally favorable materials to be found in other parts of the country which have been used in radically different forms of expression. In drawing up a survey of these domed churches, it has lately been noted that they are scattered along the Roman road which led from Rodez to Cahors and thence to Saintes by way of Périgueux and Angoulême, and was still in use during the Romanesque period. Why, however, out of all the great roads crossing medieval France used alike by pilgrims and business traffic, should this have been the only one to produce a vigorously defined architectural formula? Why did the extension of this type towards the east die out on the first slopes of the Massif Central, when the distance between Rodez and Auvergne, the Velay and the Mediterranean regions is really no more than that covered by the western section of the old road? This theory of the road is no more than approximate and does not explain the most distant manifestations of the style, lost amid many other forms, at St Hilaire in Poitiers, the abbey church of Fontevrault in Touraine, and the cathedral of Le Puy. Just as with the theory of regional schools, we must willingly admit its limitations which arise from the impotence of material objects faced with the desire of men to force and deflect them to suit their own purpose and designs.

## Monastic patrons, first in the field of reconstruction

However difficult it may be for us to retrace the attempts made in the course of the five hundred years following the fall of the Roman Empire to restore a building art worthy of the weighty heritage of antiquity, the resultant disconnected gropings clearly show that they did not take deep root in nourishing soil. This was quite the reverse, however, with the still sporadic and uncertain attempts made before the tenth century. Boldly and energetically guided by their great abbots, the ancient monasteries which had desparately tried to maintain civilized life within their walls during the dark ages, were among the first to be inspired by the revival. Almost every monastery from Agaune and Payerne to Tournus, Jumièges, Tours, Saintes and Conques was turned into a vast workshop evolving bold experiments. Fertilization of the soil, mutual exchanges and enlarged domains continually increased their resources. Disregarding cost, they spent vast sums on the building of churches that were quite out of proportion to their real needs, but considered that these supreme luxuries were offerings to God rather than themselves. They caused valuable materials to be brought great distances.

During his reconstruction of the abbey church of St Bénigne at Dijon, Abbot William of Volpiano boasted to his friend, the Bishop of Langres, of 'columns of marble and stone brought from many places.'

## Splendor and light of the great Romanesque churches

Unfortunately these splendors are no longer visible. Either the damage of time and mankind has done away with them, or they have been distorted by restorers. The patina of time which clothes them is also deceptive. Originally the great Romanesque churches glowed with rich materials, gilding, color and light. Their architecture reigned supreme; decorative sculpture and the statues surrounding their doors were subservient to it. The interiors of some of the churches were entirely covered with paintings, the most famous example being Saint-Savin-sur-Gartempe where the section of the vault over the main nave was modified as work proceeded. Recent restoration at the pilgrimage church of Saint-Julien at Brioude has revealed traces of strong toned colors and bold marbling effects on the pillars. There seems to have been a special liking for such magnificently colored buildings throughout Poitou, Touraine and Anjou, but the washed-out, velvety tones we now see are no more than approximations of the originals. In these regions, the extraordinary richness and liveliness of the wall paintings does not appear to be, as elsewhere, a convenient substitute for the lost art of mosaic, but a technique in its own right, accomplished, highly inventive and conforming to its own individual laws.

Bearing this in mind, the nineteenth century daubing of garlands and stars which were supposed to restore to some of the churches the warm atmosphere which had gradually been dissipated by the passing centuries, should not be condemned outright. The church of Civray in Poitou has been ruined by hideous daubs, but on the other hand, when the light fades from the naves of Civaux and Chauvigny, they are filled with a soft, mauve coloring which has its attraction. Visitors to Auvergne who admire the awe-inspiring majesty of the bare framework of the churches of Notre-Dame du Port, Orcival, St Nectaire and St Saturnin, are at first sight filled with incredulous amazement when confronted with the crimson repaintings at Issoire. Yet, with a little good will and imaginative ability, we may agree that the discoveries at Brioude possibly justify the decorative principle and good sense of the nineteenth century embellishers, even though their mechanical application may justify serious doubts.

The lack of local workshops with suitable qualifications often caused the replacement of large painted compositions by mere semblances of decoration. This uniformity was crowned, however, by the highlights of painted decoration applied to capitals and tympana, and extending to the triumphal representations of Christ in majesty surrounded by the symbols of the Evangelists in the apses. In odd corners of the church on free spaces of wall specially prepared at eye level, some imaginative artist would portray a patron saint or some edifying scene whose unexpected appearance disrupted the symmetry of the walls. This contributed to the flexible expansion of free, spontaneous life which enhanced the medieval churches and prevented them from becoming stereotyped and monotonous.

An atmosphere of light and glowing color seems to have been one of the basic spiritual needs of the Romanesque. Peter the Venerable, known for his detachment and his desire to restrict the Cluniac order to a life of asceticism, once alluded to the impression made on him by the paintings of a Cluniac chapel, 'by far the most beautiful of all churches in Burgundy.'

## Church treasuries and ornaments

This sense of delight included objets d'art, especially goldsmiths' work which was considered vital to architecture and enhanced its effect. Altars, canopies, chandeliers and lights were encrusted with gold, silver, enamel and precious stones. The miraculously preserved treasury of the abbey of Conques gives us some idea of the attraction of such riches. In the eleventh and twelfth centuries, two great abbots devoted themselves to increasing it, carrying on the tradition of the patron who, in the late tenth century, provided it with its awesome center-piece the famous 'idol.' Abbot Bégon, who completed the church, commissioned a portable altar and three reliquaries, the first in the form of a letter A, the second resembling an octagonal bell-tower, and the third a rectangular coffer enclosing the relics of the true cross sent by Pope Pascal II. The inscription on the very beautiful casket containing the relics of Ste Foy enables us to attribute it to his successor, Boniface.

Conques was not the only abbey in a position to embellish its magnificent church with so many ornaments. Every monastery, cathedral and pilgrimage shrine felt obliged to collect and ever increase a treasury which could be an outward sign of its fame. In matters of Romanesque archeology it is always essential to refer back to Cluny: here, an inventory of relics, jewels, books and liturgical ornaments taken in 1304 listed no fewer than 225 items, most of which probably date back to the Romanesque period.

# Plates

completing the 'corona' are framed by small columns and the semi-circle is covered by a half dome which contributes to the calm sense of balance.

## Conques: Abbey church of Ste Foy

67 The church and its setting. The massive galleried aisles framing the nave and transept are clearly visible; at Toulouse and Compostela these features also include the end walls of the transepts. An octagonal bell-tower surmounts the dome over the crossing and the narthex is flanked by square towers with modern pinnacles. The shortness of the nave is due to the miraculous spring below it.

68 The portal with its famous scene of the **Last Judgment** (first half of the twelfth century). The tympanum shows Christ surrounded by saints and angels one of whom is weighing souls. On the lintel (lower photograph) the elect ascend to paradise and the damned are swallowed by Leviathan.

69 The nave from the transept gallery.

70 The arcade of the gallery. The twin, round-headed bays are supported in the center by linked pairs of slim columns.

## Nevers: St Etienne

71 Elevation of the nave, typified by threefold staging: great arches surmounted by galleries with twin bays contained within semi-circular surrounds, and clerestory windows. Tunnel vault articulated by ribs falling on to half columns and buttressed by the quadrant vaults of the galleries.

72 A squinch of the dome covering the transept crossing, an example of perfect stone-cutting.

73 The semi-circular sanctuary. The elevation differs from that of the nave, but the rhythm is neither reduced nor altered. The huge arches outlining the semi-circle are raised to a great height on plain capitals. Paired round-headed wall arcades echo the apertures of the galleries. The clerestory windows

## Fontenay: Abbey church

74 The finely proportioned nave. The curve of the pointed tunnel vault exactly balances those of the arches opening to the aisles. The arrangement of masses and intervening gaps brings about a calculated interplay of light conducive to spiritual elevation.

75 The cloister. Here the rich repertory of Romanesque architecture abandons the tension of jagged forms in favour of subtle, restful curves. The basic rhythm of paired arches with small columns is only interrupted by wider bays giving access to the center courtyard.

76 Interior of the cloister showing the wide openings, the lightly pointed tunnel vault which offsets the squat design, the small paired columns, and the rich moldings.

77 One of the cloister pillars which links the Cluniac type of column and channeled pilasters. The capitals with their bold linear simplicity are typically Cistercian in style.

## Payerne: Abbey church

78 Nave and choir. The apse is appreciably earlier than the nave but gives the same feeling of a wide space bathed in light.

79 The semi-circular apse with its many windows.

80 One of the nave pillars with its strange imposts.

81 The nave. In the background, the semi-circular corbelled gallery, prototype of the one at Cluny.

82 The transept crossing with Gothic rib vault.

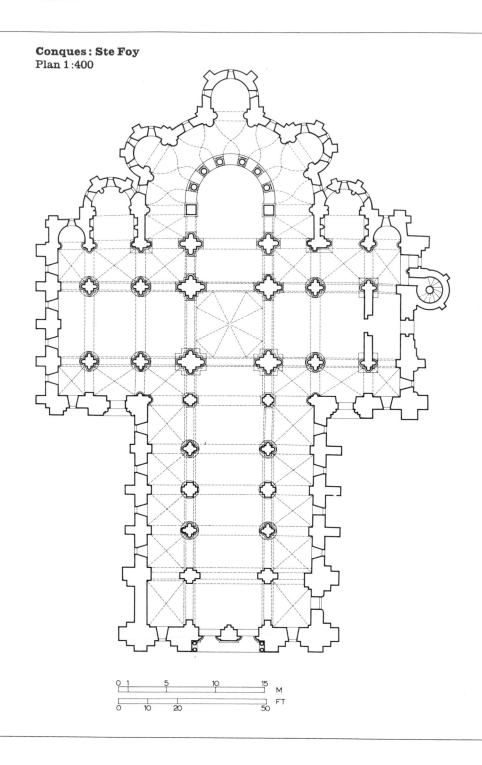

**Conques : Ste Foy**
Plan 1 :400

0 1    5    10    15
M
FT
0    10    20    50

**Nevers: St Etienne**
Plan, longitudinal section and analytical section 1:400

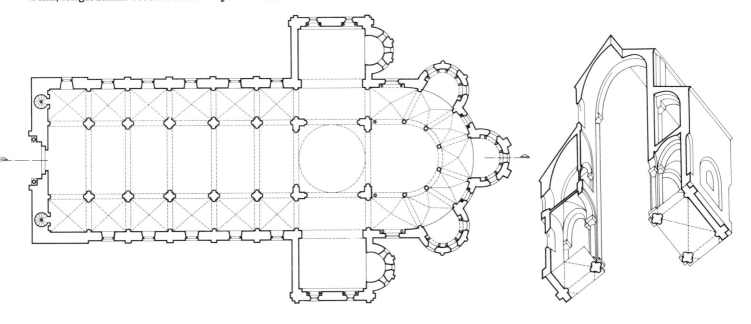

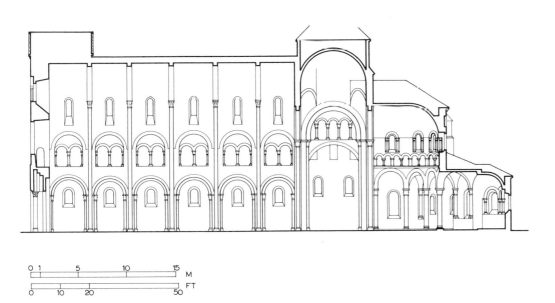

# Notes

## Conques (France): Abbey church of Ste Foy

We shall never know the real reason which led the founders of the abbey of Conques to site the monastery in one of the wildest parts of the Rouergue. Perhaps it was merely its proximity to a ford over the stream of the Dourdou in the depths of a dark gorge, combined with the presence of a spring of fresh water that later served to refresh weary pilgrims. From the tenth century onwards, the theft of the relics of Ste Foy from Agen attracted huge crowds and contributed to the prosperity of the abbey to which its priceless treasures of goldsmiths' work bear witness.

The building dates of the famous church may be problematic, but there is no doubt that it was Abbot Odolric (1030-1065) who commenced the work and probably initiated the design which was completed after his death. This consists of a narthex, a nave with aisles, transepts also with aisles, and a chevet with an ambulatory and radiating chapels. The elevation is typified by the perfect buttressing of nave, transepts and choir by galleried aisles with quadrant vaults and a large number of light openings. The same system may be found in Auvergne, at St Sernin, Toulouse, and at Compostela.

## Nevers (France): St Etienne

St Etienne was formerly the church of a Cluniac priory and was built in a single phase between 1062 and 1097. Its plan consists of a nave of six bays, a projecting transept, and a choir with ambulatory and radiating chapels. Focillon praises the unity and sober harmony of the building which owes its nobility solely to its fine composition of masses, and other critics note that it fuses Burgundian influences of tripartite elevation with those of Auvergne causing the buttressing of the central nave with its semi-circular tunnel vault by galleried aisles. It is more essential, however, to point out that the great church really owes nothing except to itself, that it exploits regional technical skills to achieve a startlingly original synthesis with the aid of one exception that still has to be explained. In order to obtain direct lighting for the nave, the architect lowered the quadrant-vaulted galleries and the keystones of the arches. This resulted in a rich, fully rounded aperture, one of the most logical frameworks ever conceived by Romanesque builders.

## Fontenay (France): Abbey

The abbey of Fontenay, founded by St Bernard, Abbot of Clairvaux, on one of his family estates in 1119, is situated in the depths of a wooded valley near Châtillon-sur-Seine in northern Burgundy. In 1139, Abbot William undertook to build a new monastery in accordance with the founder's directives. Thus Fontenay is a translation of St Bernard's architectural precepts, an admirable mixture of ascetic denudation and lofty grandeur conveyed entirely by the grouping of masses. The church was built first and consecrated by the Cistercian Pope Eugenius III in 1147. Its design is a combination of all the influences of Burgundian Romanesque architecture.

## Payerne (Switzerland): Abbey church

The chronicles credit St Odilo, Abbot of Cluny, with the rebuilding of the monastery of Payerne, newly affiliated with the Cluniac Order. According to archeologists, the major survival of this considerable undertaking is the nave of the present imposing church. This is, in fact, a building dating from the first half of the eleventh century, strongly influenced by the early Mediterranean Romanesque style but interpreting it with independent individuality. Its construction is very simple: rectangular pillars with engaged half-columns receiving the ribs of the tunnel vault, lofty arches, finely composed stonework and a complete absence of decoration. The vault is penetrated by the clerestory windows, the earliest example of this type of construction, if, indeed, it is authentic. A second phase of building began about 1050. This included the massive storeyed narthex, the seventh bay of the nave, the wide projecting transept, and a choir consisting of a huge apse flanked by four small staggered apses incorporating a timid attempt at a Cluniac pointed barrel vault.

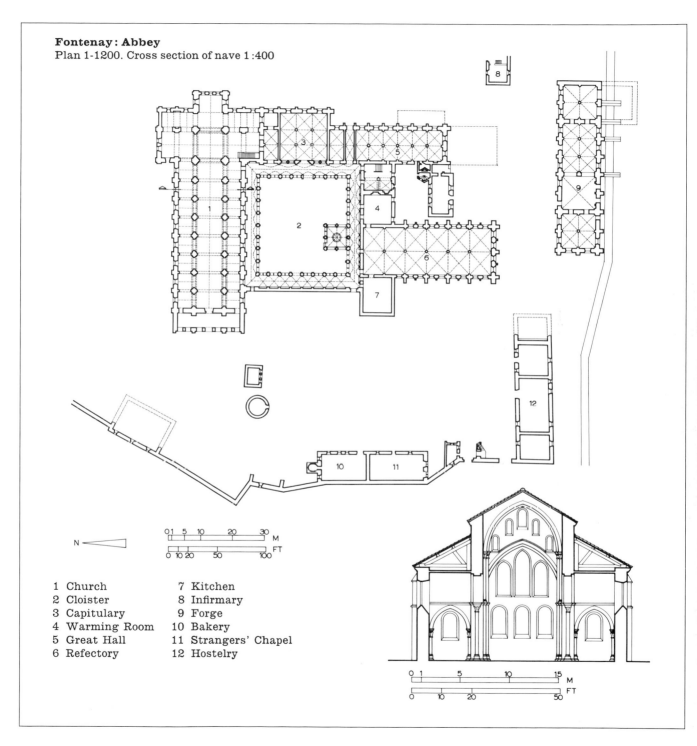

**Fontenay: Abbey**
Plan 1-1200. Cross section of nave 1:400

N

0 1 5 10 20 30 M
0 10 20 50 100 FT

1 Church
2 Cloister
3 Capitulary
4 Warming Room
5 Great Hall
6 Refectory
7 Kitchen
8 Infirmary
9 Forge
10 Bakery
11 Strangers' Chapel
12 Hostelry

0 1 5 10 15 M
0 10 20 50 FT

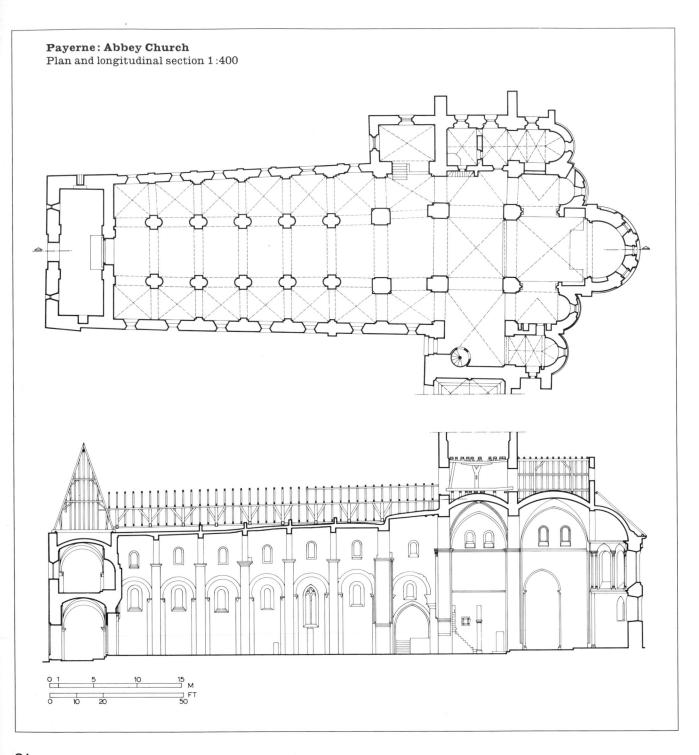

**Payerne: Abbey Church**
Plan and longitudinal section 1:400

0 1     5      10       15      M
0    10    20            50     FT

# 2. The Builders

## Popular needs

No assessment of the Romanesque world can be successful without first examining the various requirements engendered by an economic and social development which far outstripped the confines of monasteries and courts, the traditional seats of civilization. This should again be followed by an enquiry as to what degree and by what methods these needs were fulfilled. An overwhelming task, it is continually put to the test by some fresh discovery or line of approach. Though it is still scarcely possible to do more than merely indicate the main outlines of research, one finding is immediately clear. Henceforward, there were more immediate needs connected with the large towns where creative activity was based, and often dependent on them. This has its parallel today when urban expansion upsets planning programs, stimulates employment and invades the surrounding countryside. It is possible that the teeming life of the eleventh century was due to the same social and technical phenomenon. At any rate, it helps us to understand it. Towns had to be built to accommodate the new markets and, thanks to the lately found affluence, they did not merely consist of humble dwellings. The successive rebuildings of many French and Spanish towns have spared fine, carefully built private houses with wide arcades opening on to the street, and lit by arcaded galleries similar to those in the nearby churches. They were first indications of settled fortunes which continued in the same line of development. The extensive needs of the Holy Land revived all the Mediterranean ports and also created new ones. The movement of merchants, drovers and pilgrims along the reopened roads of Europe created the necessity for some form of rudimentary organization. The empiricism of the Middle Ages adapted itself to a fairly low standard, and one should be wary of the idealists who present the Romanesque pilgrimage roads as fine avenues punctuated with inns suitable for weary travelers. The excellent network of Roman roads had not survived the long centuries of invasions, and well built inns offering secure lodging were few. Later inns were not systematically linked with the needs of pilgrims and were usually run either by the two great orders of Hospitallers which had come into being thanks to the conquest of the Holy Land, or by the regular Augustinian Canons. Some of them survive, either partially or intact. They include those at Pons in Saintonge where the late twelfth century buildings adjoin the road, and at Aubrac set in the lonely countryside with a fortified chapel roofed with a fine pointed barrel vault. The more humble foundations which offered shelter and help to shepherds in the wild regions including the Pyrenees, the Massif Central and the Alps are just as moving. Architectural influences were often spread through these networks. The crossing of the little Hospitallers' church hidden in a Basque valley at Saint-Blaise is crowned by a cross-ribbed dome which derives from Moorish Spain. The tiny chapel of the hospice of Gabas founded by Gaston the Crusader in 1121 at the upper end of the wild valley of Ossau is roofed by two bays of rough, curved rib-vaults which make a singular effect in this lonely spot among the mountain streams.

The requirements of territories immersed in social and economic development are still more basic and deeply rooted. A static economy everywhere gave way to a more flexible system, linking far more closely all those who gained their livelihood from the land. This rural expansion coincided with the emergence of feudal landowners as an organized class; they acted as its protectors and guaranteed its progress. At the center of the peasant's life was the castle which was no longer merely a bulwark of defence for individuals and authority, but the secure seat of justice and administration. The number of these strongly fortified keeps rapidly increased.

Round them developed the tenants' villages which soon acquired both names and churches.

There was no longer any question of discovering building materials in remote districts and having them conveyed by water at great expense. It was necessary to build quickly, using local resources, and earth was dug and excavated for this purpose. For, in accordance with the ever increasing need, techniques which had long been the monopoly of specialized workshops established in monasteries and royal palaces, now extended to the uttermost ends of the country.

Without the vast increase in the availability of labor implicit in this undertaking, it is impossible to explain the almost countless variations of Romanesque themes. No other civilization has been so gifted in expedients and tricks of the trade. This exciting ingenuity could only have been due to craftsmen closely integrated with the society which employed them; they must have known all its secrets and its exact boundaries.

Sometimes, as at Le Puy or the Sacra di San Michele, it was a question of outlining a building on the tip of a rock, finishing off the natural landscape with the vigorously imprinted seal of the conquering faith. On the other hand, it might have to be set in a quagmire, with its functional masses set against the open sky-apse, bell-tower and nave all helping to balance one another. The excessive thickness of walls could be lightened thanks to the rhythm of arches, and a vault could be constructed which did not crush or weigh down the side walls. Massive bell-towers could be raised on a series of corbels, and buttresses distributed at the necessary points. Experience of all these problems was gained on the actual sites and then communicated and reproduced by self-taught craftsmen who knew instinctively how to solve them, paying more attention to the case in point than to the formal application of scientific theorems or accomplished working drawings.

Solutions varied in accordance with the revival of ancient usages and the suitability of materials. The blocks of granite, sandstone or basalt found in mountainous regions made for heavy, opulent buildings with full curves and robust decoration which soon took on a deadened effect. The fine volcanic limestone of the hills of western France produced a light, subtle architecture, but the most flexible combinations ranging from the domes of Périgord to the tunnel and groined vaults of Burgundy were due to the presence of thin beds of limestone. Tufa, extracted from the streams of arid mountain regions, was used in conjunction with rubble and pebbles. Regions of clay soil had no quarries but produced bricks which resulted in graceful but fragile buildings whose faded reds stand out against the green meadows and golden cornfields. The geographic distribution of Romanesque architecture with its unexpected contrasts and the charm of its individual buildings is almost wholly dependent on geological factors, on the type of subsoil available for the cheapest form of construction and transport, and on the localization of labor on the actual building sites or in their immediate neighborhood.

The emergence of this class of craftsmen shows that, in Romanesque architecture, there were no basic differences in the level of competence or expertise. The most humble chapel hidden in a valley of the Pyrenees, or by an Italian lake, was conceived and treated as an entity and so resulted in a masterpiece; its modest discoveries are appropriate, its composition engenders peace, its inspiration is inexhaustible. The Romanesque was a homogeneous style because the same talent inspired both the humblest parish churches and the greatest cathedrals.

## Architects or mere masons?

From this it might appear that Romanesque buildings were the work of laborers possessed of talent but collectively anonymous and without any pretensions to individuality, whereas Gothic architecture witnessed the revival of the master architect who was creator of the design and supreme head of the workshop. Until quite recently, Romanesque was held to be an art of masons, but contemporary judgment is fairer.

There is no doubt that Romanesque architects had little mathematical knowledge, but this was compensated by an acquired skill which, in its sheer boldness, sometimes recalls that of modern architects working with reinforced concrete. They were not trained engineers, but practical men sprung from the soil and attuned to its rhythms and its powerful empiricism. As has often been noted, to achieve the cross they used simple geometrical shapes: squares, rectangles, circles and semi-circles, renouncing the elegant but exaggerated forms of the Arab and Mozarabic styles. They made precise enlargements and adjustments with the help of symbolic combinations of figures that had been known since antiquity, though extreme caution should be exercised in checking, these on the ground today. It is fairly safe to say that Romanesque architects, like all really inspired creators, were capable of visualizing their finished buildings from the moment of their foundations being laid; they projected and outlined designs which clung to the soil and perfected the landscape. They did not hesitate to remodel and revise their plans as they worked, sometimes demolishing what they had already built if they thought the results would benefit the overall composition.

They were servants rather than masters of their designs and maintained the right to make adapations up to the completion of the work. Thus, in the early twelfth century, the choir of the Cluniac priory church of La Charité-sur-Loire was demolished, even though the preliminary work had only just been completed, and rebuilt on a grander scale, possibly because it

La-Charité-sur-Loire: Church. Ambulatory.

had been considered too small for the importance of a church which attracted so many pilgrims. At Saint-Savin-sur-Gartempe there was a still more spectacular piece of unforeseen reconstruction. Here the architect had visualized a nave with a tunnel vault supported on transverse arches, and the first three western bays were erected on these lines. The work of the fresco painter, however, seemed so promising that the chief architect apparently gave way to him and abolished all the other arches planned so that the artist could use the resulting vast expanse of wall.

Leaving aside for the moment the enormous Rhenish cathedrals and the principal pilgrimage churches which excite so much admiration today, there are many well-known buildings of secondary importance which have so much individuality that it is almost impossible to deny the hand of an undisputed master architect. To take a single example from the countless ones available: the choir of the church of Châteaumeillant in Bérry. This does its anonymous builder great credit with its striking array of seven apses and its airy combinations of twin pierced arches supported on slim columns so that they communicate with one another. To take a more famous example, the cloister at Moissac with its assured composition, its harmonious succession of slim single and double columns, and its sequence of identical splayed capitals, denotes first and foremost the proved skill of a talented yet modest architect who did not see fit to leave his name to posterity on the inscription commemorating the actual building.

It is equally annoying to be unable to attach any architect's name to the amazing abbey church of Charroux in Poitou. Before its wanton destruction, this must have been one of the most perfect and original of all Romanesque achievements. The Benedictine abbey of Charroux was founded in the second half of the eighth century and

Moissac: Cloister. Elevation.

became famous on account of the council which was held there in 989 in an attempt to bring about the Peace of God; it also possessed a treasury of holy relics some of which had actually been handled by Christ. To house these and present them with due solemnity to worshipping pilgrims, an exceptionally ambitious building program was devized, involving an audacious blend of the two seemingly incompatible plans inherited by the Romanesque world: the cruciform basilica and the rotunda. So far, these two traditional designs had either been treated separately or simply juxtaposed. It was left to the unknown architect of Charroux in the first third of the eleventh century to realize their organic combination by inserting a vast rotunda in the heart of his building, at the crossing. Here there was a central space from which pilgrims could look

down on the relics in the crypt; this was bounded by eight four-lobed pillars and extended by a triple ambulatory which decreased in height. Wide transepts with small apses on their eastern sides projected to north and south, and a semi-circular chevet, probably with small radiating apses, prolonged the rotunda to the east. Worshippers entering the nave must have been struck by the immense height of the crossing which was filled with light penetrating through the numerous bays. A double system of superimposed arches surrounded the central space with its raised altar, the lower ones acting as supports. At ground level the plan was circular, but higher up became octagonal to receive the segments of the lofty tunnel vaults over the first of the ambulatories. Unfortunately, all that survives of this impressive and unique building is the lantern-tower dominating the squat roofs of the now small, sleepy town.

## Some names on the stone

Too many extravagant deductions have been drawn from the frequent, but by no means systematic habit of anonymity to be worth while making a point of it here (apart from the fact that there is too little documentation on the subject).

First it is necessary to distinguish between the administrator of the works and the technician responsible for the direction of the workshop, and the teams of quarrymen, builders and decorators. This is something which the few surviving contemporary texts do not always specify. Of these the Chronicle of St Bénigne concerning the rebuilding of the Benedictine abbey church at Dijon shortly after 1100 is one of the most valuable in references on this point. The Latin terms which it freely employs show that the direction of the undertaking was divided between two authorities. The Bishop of Langres, who initiated the restoration of the ancient monastery, was in charge of the financial administration, and organized the transport of materials to the site. To Abbot William fell the twofold task of 'specifying the work itself' and 'directing the laborers.' The latter term barely admits discussion; it takes for granted that the Abbot must have possessed the grasp of architecture implied by the first definition. The fame of the workshop set up by Abbot William spread beyond the boundaries of Burgundy; for the Abbot of Fécamp requested him to provide him with craftsmen ('artifices') who would be able to complete the monastery buildings which he had begun.

Not all textual references or the evidence of actual names have the same significance. Quite often it is merely a question of a name clumsily carved on a stone. Many Romanesque capitals in Spain, Italy and France bear signatures, but all these unexplained names raise inexplicable problems. We must strongly beware of making identifications which cannot really be authenticated. On the doorway of the cathedral at Ferrara may be found the signature of Master Nicolo, one of the first identified sculptors of Romanesque Italy. His work shows Byzantine influence, but his individual talent endows his carvings with dramatic realism. He may have been responsible for the fine reliefs on the façade of San Zeno at Verona, but his identification with the Nicolo who, in 1135, signed a capital in the Sacra di San Michele in Piedmont is by no means certain.

## 'Gislebertus hoc fecit'

On the other hand, it is certainly Abbot William, the rebuilder of St Bénigne at Dijon, after the fire of 1137, who is named in the rhyming inscriptions surrounding the two tympana of the building, now preserved in the Archeological Museum in the city. Such examples bring us to what is probably the most famous signature in Romanesque art: 'Gislebertus hoc fecit.' This is proudly placed at the feet of the figure of Christ in the Last Judgment set above the west door of the Cathedral of St Lazare at Autun. Gislebertus was a very common name during this period and contemporary texts quote several in southern Burgundy alone. This one is usually regarded as the gifted sculptor of the composition above the west door and of the greater proportion of the interior's highly individual capitals. The sculptor has even been called the Cézanne of the Romanesque, an attractive, though dangerously equivocal idea. Whereas Cézanne, at the heart of the Impressionist revival, opened the way to the development of contemporary painting, Gislebertus, in 1130, witnessed the last rays of Romanesque supremacy; moreover, behind him, was the overwhelming weight of the inheritance of Cluny from which he never dared to completely free himself.

For those with some experience of the psychology of the Middle Ages, it would be dishonest to agree to this identification without a certain degree of reserve. It has never been definitely proved that the word 'hoc' refers to the sculpture above the portal and, by extension, to the sculptures of the church as a whole which are clearly the work of the same hand apart from a few details. This brevity and imprecision, compared with the inscriptions at Dijon, might allow it to refer to the entire building to which the portal is no more than a vestibule, connecting it with either the architect, the surveyor of the works, or some clerk or chaplain of the bishop's entourage responsible for the direction of the undertaking. In fact, while the shrine was building, a 'Gislebertus cappelanus' is recorded as having witnessed a donation made to a canon of the Cathedral of Autun in the presence of the bishop, Etienne de Bâgé. This hypothesis cannot be proved. In this connection it may be recalled that the name 'Turold' which occurs in the last verse of the 'Song of Roland' has still received no definite explanation. It will probably be a long time before we know whether this name represents an immortal poet, a minstrel singing the lays of others, or a copyist who transcribed the Oxford manuscript.

## Cluny

From Tournus, roads run over the flat-topped limestone hills of the Mâconnais to Cluny which also had close connections with the abbey of St Bénigne at Dijon. Moreover, it was the art of Cluny which was transmitted across the forests northwards to Autun to inspire the architecture of the cathedral of St Lazare and influence the work of the gifted sculptor, Gislebertus.

Throughout the eleventh century the liturgical life of the great abbey unfolded against the background of the church begun by Abbot Aymard, probably after 948, and consecrated during the period of office of Abbot Mayeul in 981. This building, dating from the very end of the pre-Romanesque period, was certainly important even though by no means a masterpiece. Basilican in plan, its nave of seven bays was unvaulted, flanked by aisles, and cut by a narrow transept which projected widely from the body of the church, each arm ending in a small semi-circular apse. The deep-set choir had pillars and a semi-circular apse flanked by two small apses which protruded from the straight walls. Between the choir aisles which gave access to these chapels and the small apses at the ends of the transepts were inserted two long rectangular rooms divided by interior partitions and linked by narrow passages either with the transepts or the sanctuary. The composition freely developed the monumental plan of graded apses, known as Benedictine on account of its frequent, though not exclusive, use by this order. Romanesque architects derived some fine effects from it. The nave at Cluny was preceded by a narthex or galilee which heralded the beautiful closed porches flanked by towers which were the work of the following generation.

Building was resumed by Abbot Odilo who did not limit his activity to Cluny but devoted himself to many churches elsewhere, including Payerne, Charlieu, Ambierle-en-Forez, Ris and Sauxillanges in Auvergne, Souvigny, Saint-Saturnin-du-Port in Provence, and Lavoûte-sur-Allier which he founded on one of his own estates and later became the starting point of one of the routes to Santiago. At Cluny he devoted his final years to the building of a beautiful cloister, but first 'restored all the interiors, except for the walls of the church:' it is thought that he had a stone vault constructed, replacing the timber roof (though this may be a false conclusion drawn from his biographer, Jotsaud).

Cluny: Abbey church of SS Peter and Paul. Reconstruction of choir after K. J. Conant.

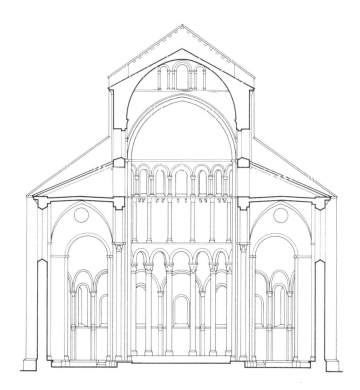

This church, a little less than 150 feet long, was sufficient for the needs of a medium sized community. The continual growth in number of the brethren in the course of the eleventh century rendered it too small, however, and Abbot Hugh of Semur was forced to envisage not merely rebuilding and extension, but the construction on the grounds to the north, of an abbey church surpassing all those of Western Christendom in size. A heavy annual tribute drawn from the kings of Spain assured the financing of the undertaking conceived as the outward manifestation of the power of the head of the order. Seen against the background of the Roman Church, such a proposition would not have appeared as out of proportion as it does to us, forcibly accustomed as we are to more modest religious programs. Nevertheless, the abbot apparently had to bear the stigma of pride and megalomania and was forced to justify the excessive dimensions of his new church. The design with its nave of eleven bays flanked by double aisles to balance its length, its two transepts and ambulatory with small radiating apses was so magnificent as to earn it the name of 'the angel's walk.' St Hugh's abbey church was to remain the pride of the Cluniac order for seven hundred years.

## Saint-Benoît-sur-Loire

Just as today, rivalry between artists was one of the basic sources of creative activity. Even the most incorruptible churchmen were affected by it, and there were several instances of durable masterpieces originating from the opposition of two proud and ambitious clerics. When, at St Benoît-sur-Loire, the head of Abbot Gaucelin's technicians asked him what type of work they would have to undertake, the abbot proudly replied: 'Let it be such as to be an example to the whole of France.' The compiler of the Latin 'Life of Gaucelin,' who tells this story, describes this surveyor of the works as 'princeps artific-

Saint-Benoît-sur-Loire: Abbey church. Elevation of tower-porch.

um,' meaning prince of technicians. He must have been an individual of importance and talent to be admitted into the confidence of his patron, the abbot. It is asking too much, however, to identify him with the 'Umbertus' of the capital: there may be nothing to strictly invalidate this theory but, on the other hand, there is nothing to authenticate it. However, this may be, the admirable result of his work still remains: a monumental tower-porch whose overall conception is clearly his. Incidentally, this shows up the falsity of the method adopted by archeologists of regulating the chronology of Romanesque buildings by the periods of office of bishops or abbots. The exact part played by Gaucelin in the construction of the great church is a matter of dispute, but the fact that he died before the building was finished was of slight importance as the architect survived him long enough to assure its completion.

## The Cathedral of Compostela: a bishop, a treasurer, a superintendent of the works, an assistant and fifty stone-cutters

A short time before, in the eleventh century, the cathedral of Compostela was enlarged as the result of a threefold collaboration. Bishop Diego Peláez who occupied the see from 1070 to 1088 decided to rebuild the basilica commissioned by Alfonso the Great in the late ninth century, devasted by the raider Almanzor and restored by Alfonso V. The general direction of the work was entrusted to qualified representatives of the cathedral chapter, one of whom, Bernard, known as the Old, was responsible for the plan. According to the 'Pilgrims' Guide' which has left us a valuable description of the great cathedral, he was assisted by a deputy named Robert and about fifty stone-cutters. The guide describes him as a stonemason, thus giving fresh proof of the overlapping of technical functions within a workshop, and awards him the title of 'mirabilis

magister.' It also calls him 'domnus,' which leads to the belief that he may have been a clerk, many of whom, in the opinion of archeologists, were of French origin. Certainly the name Bernard is not a familiar one in the Spanish language. Others identify him with the Bernard who was treasurer of the chapter and was responsible for the monumental fountain which greeted pilgrims from France on the square to the north of the basilica. However this may be, he was possessed of a lively, eclectic talent and worked on the churches of St Martial at Limoges, Sainte-Foy at Conques and St Sernin at Toulouse. Master Stephen also worked on the site at Santiago with such excellent results that, in 1101, he was requested to provide plans for the cathedral at Pampeluna.

Similar organization was favored for the building of the fine Cluniac priory at Montierneuf at Poitiers. Under the command of Prior Guy, who was the nephew of St Hugh and may well have modeled himself on his uncle as patron and builder, the work was directed by a monk named Ponce, assisted by Mainard, a master-mason or stone-cutter. This building was not begun until 1077, but the church was either finished or very near completion on its consecration less than twenty years later in 1096.

## Glory to God through assembled stones

Only very rarely does one find detailed information regarding the careers of laymen in Romanesque writings. Their contemporaries seldom bothered to hand down to posterity the names of the creators of the masterpieces which so delighted them. Besides, we must realize that, very often, the dazzling personality of the patron outshone those of the technicians under his command and that, to contemporary eyes, his pious intention of acting as intermediary with God and his angels surpassed the merits of the execution.

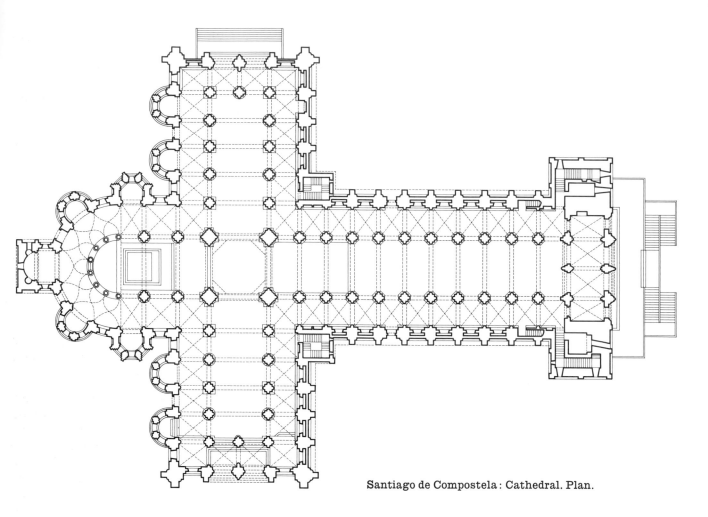

Santiago de Compostela: Cathedral. Plan.

The saintliness of his soul was expressed in the splendor seen to clothe God's house. Peter the Venerable, Abbot of Cluny, contemplating Suger's work at St Denis exclaimed: 'This man who does not build for himself, but for God alone, this man covers us with shame!' The slightest trace of personal gratification had to be barred from the consecrated building; on the other hand, total involvement in the building and its decoration, and passionate rivalry in its conception and in the choice of foremen, laborers and materials, meant working for the transcendence of God for which nothing was too much or too dear. Romanesque art is distinguished by these chain reactions; it may not always be inventive, but it transforms.

## A symbolic architecture: the circular plan

Thus, Abbot Williams of Volpiano borrowed the plan of a rotunda grafted to the chevet of a basilican-type church from a pre-Romanesque formula fairly frequently used in Burgundy. He applied it to the church of St Bénigne at Dijon, where it became more or less taken for granted.

94

Nevertheless, the scale it conferred to the building, the monumental three tiered elevation, and the superimposed columns were all due to the abbot and it would be unfair to grudge him credit for this. In the thirteenth century, the Norwegians built a 'Gothic version' above the tomb of St Olaf at Trondheim. It is significant, too, that, about the same time, another illustrious patron, Abbot Oliba of St Michel de Cuxa adapted the same idea for his own use. Like William of Volpiano, he had inherited an impressive pre-Romanesque church built in the Visigothic tradition. The abbey was richly endowed with relics, particularly those which had been brought there by Pietro Orseolo, the former Doge of Venice, and in the early years of the eleventh century, was an influential center. So much so, that it sent one of its brethren who was an architect to St Martin du Canigou where he built a church which was consecrated in 1009. Abbot Oliba was himself the son of the Count of Barcelona and the most influential counselor of the King of Navarre who, acting on his advice, inquired into the reforms of the Cluniacs and was indirectly responsible for their introduction to Spain. His sphere of influence extended as far as St Benoît-sur-Loire. At Cuxa, he enclosed the existing sanctuary with a large chevet with an ambulatory and enlarged the church to the west with a group of buildings 'of admirable workmanship:' these have come to light in recent excavations. Jean Hubert has shown that their core was a tiered rotunda directly evocative of those in far away Burgundy.

The talent of these builders, with their developed sense of balance, was molded by so many relevant symbols and touches of allusion whose meanings are now lost, that it may be necessary to look for another, more subtle, explanation for the adoption of such an unusual plan in a southern setting. In fact, Romanesque architects never abandoned the central, or more specifically, circular plan which they inherited from Roman buildings. Reinterpreted and enriched, it survived the pre-Romanesque period, associated either with funerary themes or with nostalgia for the Holy Sepulcher at Jerusalem. Perhaps the most perfect and original evocation of this memory is the massive rotunda of Neuvy-St-Sépulcre which the Chronicle of Limoges quotes as resembling the Holy Sepulcher; it consists of a round sanctuary enclosed by a colonnade and a circular ambulatory. This promenade is surmounted by a gallery with semi-circular arches opening on to the central space. Thus distributed in the West, the model of the Holy Sepulcher reached as far as Denmark, where, according to K. J. Conant, round churches constituted an interesting episode in the medieval architecture of the country; the island of Bornholm has no fewer than four important and typical examples. They were probably inspired by the great pilgrimage made by King Sigurd the Great to the Holy Land between 1107 and 1111.

At Cuxa, the idea of a circular crypt dedicated to the Virgin, known as the Crypt of the Crib, may have been inspired by the church of the Nativity at Bethlehem which consisted of a sanctuary in an octagonal chevet linked to a rectangular nave with double aisles. There may, however, have been still another unconscious influence behind this plan. Cuxa was not the only place in the eleventh and twelfth centuries where the cult of the Archangel Michael was for a short time associated with buildings of circular or central plan without interior colonnades. The strange yet beautiful church of St Michel d'Entraygues in Charente, built in 1137 to welcome and restore needy pilgrims on their way to Santiago, consists of a perfect octagon with a small apse attached to each wall. At St Michel d'Aiguilhe in Velay the central plan oratory of 962 was surrounded in the eleventh century with a roughly oval ambulatory whose irregular design can only be explained by the shape of the narrow terrace on which the chapel is perched at the summit of a volcanic rock. It is certainly worthy of its position and presents one of the boldest expressions of building construction ever achieved by Romanesque masons, a result which was undoubtedly assisted by geological factors. There is no such explanation, however, for the strange little circular crypt of the church of the Commandery of St Michel de Mifaget on the French side of the Pyrenees a little distance from Cuxa, which was founded by the Hospitallers of Le Somport on the road at the foot of the mountains leading to Oloron from Bagnères, Lourdes and St Pé de Bigorre. The plan of this small building, half buried in the ground, is reduced to linear perfection: it is a complete circle entered by a staircase set in the last bay of the north side of the nave and is roofed by a small flattened dome, constructed of fine regular

St Michel d'Entraigues (Charente): Church. Circular plan, an example of symbolic architecture.

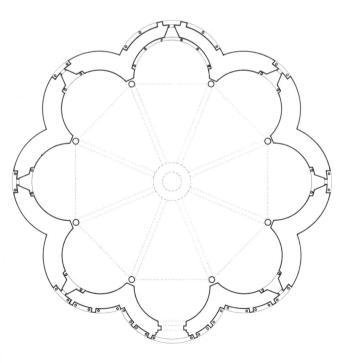

stones. Three small round-headed windows are hollowed in the east side, and a continuous bench surrounds the bottom of the wall. From outside it offers no distinctive feature and the eastern half blends with the semi-circular apse built above it.

The secondary importance of the Commandery, the small scale of its church and the absence of any special form of worship or pilgrimage in this place did not call for a development of this kind derived from pre-Romanesque churches with rounded chevets. The name of the church may, however, supply an enticing explanation. The pure design of the circular portion and the cupola clearly recall some of the funerary buildings of ancient Rome and we may well wonder if, in fact, they were inspired by the famous Mausoleum of Hadrian on the right bank of the Tiber, now more usually known as the Castel Sant'Angelo. A famous episode relating to the cult of St Michael, which had a great hold over the medieval imaginaton, is connected with this building. In the time of Pope Gregory the Great the city was ravaged by a terrible plague which had already carried off the Pope's predecessor, Pelagius. The story goes that, during the solemn processions decreed by Gregory to implore the clemency of heaven, the Pope beheld the Archangel appear as a dazzling vision on the summit of the huge building and return his sword to its sheath. The general conclusion drawn from this was that the scourge, merited for the sins of mankind, would soon come to an end. In gratitude for the miracle, Gregory's successor, Pope Boniface IV, caused a chapel and statue of the Archangel to be erected above the building so as to be seen from all over the city. The statue was made of marble and survived until the eighteenth century when it was replaced by the present bronze.

The exact ways by which the memory of this stirring event reached the humble foundation in the Pyrenees remain unknown, but the connection seems obvious and quite in keeping with what is known of Romanesque psychology.

## Churches with series of domes

It is impossible to apply similar arguments based on symbolism to other forms of architectural transmission of even greater significance. Instead, intellectual relationships and mysterious associations of temperament and taste embedded in individual souls intervened to produce other astonishing types of building. This appears to have been so particularly in the case of the churches with series of domes which are found in part of Aquitaine. We already know about the attempts to explain these with reference to roads and geological factors. Quite recently, however, it has been realized that the chief reason for the emergence and spread of this highly original formula may well have been due to human influence.

One of the most famous examples of these churches is undoubtedly the pilgrimage shrine of St Front at Périgueux which was ruthlessly restored by Abadie in the nineteenth century. Similarities in the construction of its domes have often been noted with the oldest of those roofing the near-by Cathedral of St Etienne-de-la-Cité; chief of these is the curious system of ashlar merely covered with stucco. St Etienne also provides analogies with the cathedral of Angoulême, another church vaulted with a series of domes. These would be extraordinary were it not known that Bishop Girard de Blaye who rebuilt the cathedral in the early twelfth century had for a long time been director of the college at Périgueux and still maintained close relations with the chapter of St-Etienne-de-la-Cité. Girard was the contemporary of Géraud III de Cardaillac, Bishop of Cahors (1109-1112), who undertook the rebuilding of his cathedral after his return from a pilgrimage to the Holy Land.

Périgueux: St Front (after a nineteenth century engraving).

While in the East he must have been struck by many Byzantine churches roofed with several domes which, elsewhere in the West, had inspired the builders of St Mark's in Venice. His model would have been the Church of the Holy Apostles at Constantinople, now destroyed. In the late twelfth century, the airy, elegant system of three lofty circular cupolas set over the nave on Persian-type squinches was adopted at San Cataldo in Palermo.

A similar device was adopted by the Bishop of Cahors for his cathedral. As for its chronology, not too much should be made of the date of

July 27, 1119, which is sometimes given as that of the consecration. In actual fact this only refers to the individual dedications of the high altar and the altar of the Holy Shroud by Pope Calixtus II on his way back from the Council of Toulouse. One should rather concentrate on the surprising effect of the two huge domes which weigh down on the interior so pleasingly finished off by the wide semi-circle of the chevet preserved from the eleventh century. Their swelling curves represent more than the functional needs of a well articulated building housing a ritual which had to be visible to the entire congregation. The setting of great domes on pendentives balanced merely at their four corners achieves a delicacy not found in basilican architecture and seems to correspond to the bishop's desire to create an original building – to which end he exhorted his technicians to abandon conventional methods.

René Crozet has investigated the relationships connecting some of these builders, which clearly played a very large part in the diffusion and repetition of such a powerfully defined formula. One of the most significant was the close friendship between Girard de Blaye and Robert d'Arbrissel, founder of the Abbey of Fontevrault. Robert was an extreme ascetic and an impassioned preacher of absolute repentance, by no means a man to admit the expensive luxury of a great architectural design for his church unless it had been externally imposed on him by some considered feeling of gratitude or a disinterested offer of justification. His abbey church of Fontevrault was consecrated in 1119 by Pope Calixtus II: it is vaulted by a series of domes which would be quite inexplicable were it not for these connections, as the Abbey is situated well to the north of the area covered by building of this type, in the heart of a region where completely different styles prevail.

The adoption of a series of domes to vault the wide nave of the pilgrimage church of St Hilaire at Poitiers was due to a similar type of transmission; otherwise it is rare to find this system used in Poitou. This case was different, however, in that it was merely a question of applying it to a pre-existing building created through the patronage of Queen Emma of England, and continued by Agnes, Countess of Poitou; its dedication was celebrated on November 1, 1049. Walter Coorland, a Norman or English architect, was responsible for the early plans which only ran to a timber vault or flat ceiling over the nave; this was designed to be very wide so as to accommodate a gathering of pilgrims visiting the tomb of the saint. One of the texts of the 'Miracles of St Hilaire' discloses that the builders were concerned a few years later with replacing this form of roof with a stone vault 'as much to avoid the danger of fires as out of anxiety to make the building more of a unity.' This rebuilding is dated to the early years of the twelfth century and supposedly involved the reduction of the nave bays to a square plan by the insertion of slender four-lobed pillars designed to receive the domes; between these and the former arched nave walls were spaces which amounted to narrow aisles. This has not been wholly substantiated, however, because the nave fell into a ruinous state and was only reconstructed in 1869 on the approximate pattern of the last, sole surviving bay.

Unlike the domed churches of Angoumois and Saintonge, there was no question here of a creative stroke conceived in the first flush of freedom; it was an empirical device capable of adjustment to an early building without doing it any harm. By directing the thrusts to the four corners of each bay, domes restricted the danger of the construction falling out of alignment and of excessive pressure on the arched walls. As work proceeded, however, the builders became aware of the necessity to support them, and this was done by the device of semi-circular arches applied later. The domes were mounted on squinches, a method traditionally used in the district of Poitiers, despite what has been said to the contrary; this system presented the builders with no particular problem, as they were used to employing it at the crossings of their churches.

Thus it is by no means essential to direct attention to the possible influence of the cathedral of Le Puy where the bays of the nave are roofed by a series of six domes. Historical connections certainly existed, however, between Poitiers and Le Puy, as the relics of St Hilaire were removed to the latter place for safety during the Norman invasions of the tenth century; there they were to be gradually forgotten until their rediscovery in 1655. At Le Puy, however, the exciting impression produced by a series of lofty domes, four of which rest on pointed arches, is merely the result of an extension realized in at least two stages during the twelfth century. The original nucleus consisting of the chevet, transept, and two eastern bays of the nave, was radically altered in the nineteenth century. The domes over the third and fourth bays were the only ones to escape restoration and are completely different in construction from those at Poitiers on account of the addition of a spacious colonnaded drum which has the effect of raising them aloft into a mysterious world of shadows. To agree that there is a stylistic connection between Le Puy and St Hilaire merely begs the question and does not solve it; for the origin of the domes of Le Puy is still unknown. Arab influence has often been alleged, but this by no means explains everything.

The dating of the vaults of St Hilaire, based on a chronologically vague account in the 'Miracles,' varies between 1110 and 1130. The building of domed churches in Angoumois and Saintonge had then reached its height, and it would have been odd if some slight echo of this had not reached Poitiers. The diocese of Poitiers, like those of Angoulême, Saintes and Périgueux, formed part of western Aquitaine whose capital was Bordeaux, and this resulted in reciprocal connections in the interior of a province which elsewhere was constantly traversed by pilgrims to Santiago who took the great road to the west from Paris and St Martin at Tours. Thus the masons of Poitiers adopted an idea which flourished in their vicinity but considered that it was more convenient to use squinches in the narrow spandrels of the arches supporting the domes, in place of elongated pendentives.

Absolute freedom of design is no more than an invention of a few modernists. The minds of the Romanesque builders were free of all academic theories and prejudices; for them it was the need of the living building with its constant remodelings which brought about the most original solutions. This was the case at Tournus where it has been ascertained that the problem was very similar to that at St Hilaire. When Abbot Peter I (1066-1105) decided to cover the Lombard-style nave with a stone roof, it was discovered that the slim, lofty columns would not bear the weight of a continuous cylindrical vault. Taking inspiration from the narthex which offers a sample of all the vaulting systems used by Romanesque architects before the discovery of the semi-circular tunnel vault, the builders adopted the highly ingenious device of parallel transverse tunnel vaults on diaphragm arches, a system which also allowed a clerestory. The large scale clerestory windows, probably foreseen in the original plan, admit a pale, ochreous light to play on the scoured stone pillars of the nave.

## From ascetism and denial to total architecture: Fontenay

We must return to the most powerful intellectual genius of the twelfth century at the very end of the Romanesque period to assemble its contributions into a synthesis which is all the more affecting as being a highly characteristic example of a mental ideal accurately transposed into architecture. Unfortunately, history has not left us with the name of the architect of the wonderful abbey of Fontenay hidden in the depths of a wooded valley near Châtillon-sur-Seine in Upper Burgundy. All we know is the name of the abbot who founded this magnificent, austere building: the ascetic Bernard of Clairvaux. Though an exact contemporary of Abbot Suger of St Denis he was his complete opposite. Bernard of Clairvaux opposed Suger's attachment to sensual display, just as he had prohibited the colored illumination of manuscripts so loved by his master, St Stephen Harding, Abbot of Cîteaux. In the 'Apology to William of St Thierry' he wrote violently against any form of luxury in monastic life, and this could similarly be applied to the fantastic, imaginative scrolls of early Cistercian miniatures.

The windy, deserted wastelands of the Burgundian plateau and the marshy plains of Cîteaux left an indelible mark on him. He was not so much an enemy of art, as a rediscoverer of the supreme end of architecture: not only fusion with the natural landscape but the spiritual harmony of those who inhabit it.

The danger of extreme ascetism in architecure – and this is equally applicable today – lies in the eventual reduction of the gap which should separate an ecclesiastical from a secular building; the former may be so devalued that it will appear indistinguishable from a fine barn, both architectural effects appearing similar. Bernard of Clairvaux's ideal church can only be saved by the double principle according to which his genius established it. Thus it does not matter that his basic premise rests on the arbitrary opinion that the attraction of sensual beauty deflects the worshipping monks from their prayers instead of accompanying them as a discreet counterpoint in their search for God. Based on spiritual values, Cistercian architecture is entirely sincere esoteric.

Abbot William of Fontenay, assisted by the patronage of Bishop Everard of Norwich, embarked on the building of the Monastery on its present site in 1139, just one year before the solemn consecration of the narthex of St Denis. The church was constructed without interruption and consecrated by Pope Eugenius III on September 21, 1147. There is a great deal of historical evidence to indicate that the architect's hand was directed to produce an extremely loyal interpretation of St Bernard's spiritual beliefs. The church borrows gratuitously from the vast repertory of Burgundian architecture, thereby realizing an amazing concentration of style. From Cluny come the fine pointed tunnel vault strengthened by extremely simple transverse ribs and the striking perforation of the wall connecting the nave with the lower choir. Tournus provides the mutually supporting transverse tunnel vaults roofing the aisles and chapels, allowing the buttresses to be reduced to the slenderest proportions. Finally, the nave deprived of direct lighting derives from an eleventh century tradition: light glides through the aisle windows and streams in triangular shafts from the opposing bays of the façade and chevet. Here, form is paramount. Fontenay seems as vast as the surrounding forest; yet its actual measurements are astonishing. The total length is barely 200 feet, half that of Cluny, and the interior height 42 feet compared with 66 at Conques and 90 at Cluny. Comparing it with Fontenay and the Royal Abbey of St Denis, both strictly contemporary and contradictory in appearance, we may appreciate the almost infinite richness of a repertory able to offer the austere power of the former and the brilliant magic of the latter with its translucent gems.

# Plates

## Almenno San Bartolomeo: San Tomaso in Lemine

105 This pilgrimage shrine dating from the eleventh century shows that the adoption of a circular plan by Romanesque architects was not reserved for buildings taking their name from the Holy Sepulcher. The design is perfectly regular and the plain cylindrical surface is only enlivened by the interplay of Lombard type arcading. The building is crowned by two contracted masses of similar shape which look as if they are inserted into the base. The terminal lantern resembles a North Italian campanile.

106 The round cupola with its light openings and the galleries of the ambulatory opening on to it with wide round-headed bays resting on columns with richly-worked capitals.

107 One of the groined vaults of the gallery showing traces left by the primitive scaffolding.

## Tuscania: San Pietro

108 The interior with its hypostyle nave, range of clerestory windows and uniform timber roof only relieved by the lower semi-dome of the apse is a noteworthy survival of an Early Christian basilica.

109 One of the great arches of the nave with its strange projecting keystones. Note the Ionic capital, timber roof and narrow aisle windows.

110 The crypt looking towards the nave.

111 The apsidal chevet of the crypt with its forest of columns.

## Portonovo: Santa Maria

112 The choir ambulatory seen from the side-aisle from which it is separated by arches carried on columns.

113 The nave, the transept crossing surmounted by a dome on squinches, choir and apse. Uniform tunnel vaulting with indirect lighting of the nave.

114 The oval dome over the crossing emphasised by a cornice with plain modillions. The drum is lit by twin arched openings on each side of its four sides and the squinches are terminated by horizontal slabs.

115 Detail of the nave.

## Monteriggioni

116 Set in a landscape as desolate as Castile, the walls spread like a ribbon round the flattened summit of the hill. The rectangular towers, seldom found in such fortifications, are twice as high as the wall and resemble those of a fortified Arab village.

117 Detail of the fortified wall.

## Alpirsbach: Abbey

118 The transept crossing and detail of a carving at the base of a pillar.

119 General view showing the articulation of the un-vaulted masses and the four powerful diaphragm arches of the crossing which form the focal point of the interior.

120 The massive westwork.

## Maria-Laach: Abbey church

121 General view of the exterior showing the chevet. Apse with arcaded gallery. Lombard-type turrets, octagonal tower over the crossing.

122 The massive westwork with its rounded towers.

123 The nave, for comparison with Alpirsbach. Diaphragm arches are extended throughout its length.

124 The highly developed capitals of the portal.

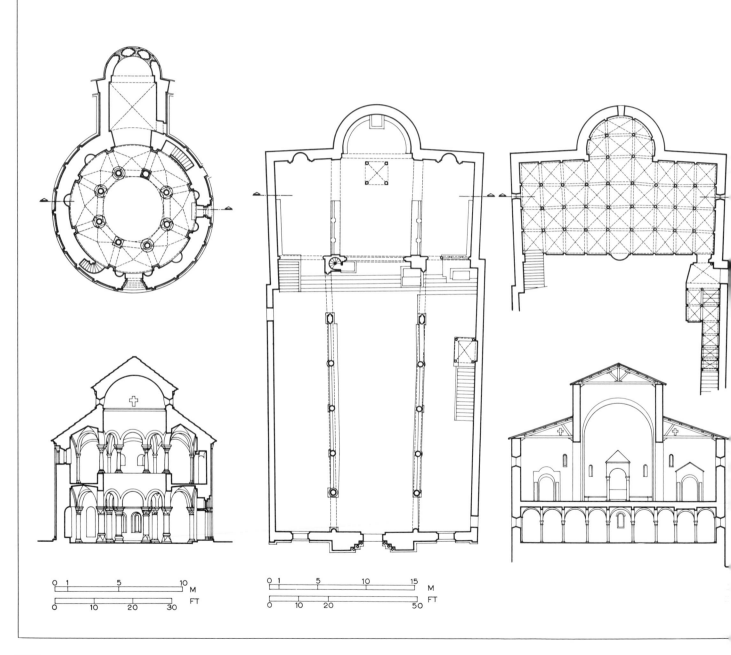

**Almenno S Bartolomeo : S Tomaso**
Plan and cross section 1 : 300

**Tuscania : S Pietro**
Plan, plan of crypt and cross section 1 : 400

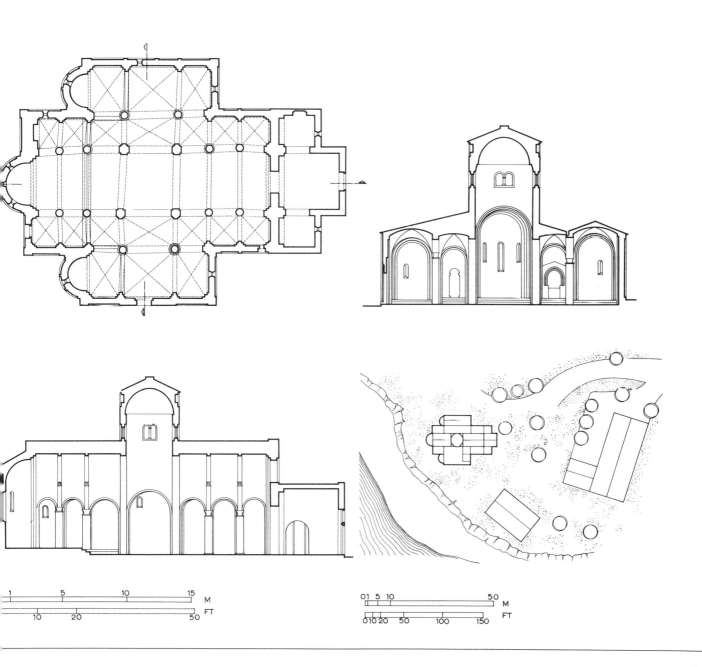

# Notes

## Italy

It would be quite wrong to exclude Italy from the Romanesque world as has sometimes been suggested, under the pretext that the peninsula containing the great basilicas of Constantine, enlivened by its connections with Byzantium and subject to the influence of Islamic art in the south, would not have been responsive to an architectural style in opposition to its individual genius. It is true that, in Italy more than anywhere else, the Romanesque style was widely influenced by the solid heritage of Roman classicism, nor could the architects of Como ever conceal their debt to Ravenna. Moreover, political discords and changes, the rivalry between individual cities, and the attraction of the Near East with which the Italian ports conducted trade, all prevented the development and establishment of artistic centers sufficiently defined to acquire universal currency. Nevertheless, these diverse influences from north, south, east and, presently, from France, which invaded the cities and provinces of Italy, were sufficient to bring about astonishing architectural syntheses often combining contradictory styles. The most outstanding, but not the only example, are the mixed styles of the cathedrals of Sicily. Nevertheless, the expression of Romanesque in Italy was not limited to these amazing hybrids. The examples illustrated here show to what extent artists and architects yielded to a real spirit of inventiveness characterized by an inner feeling for design and a mature sense of balance between the tension of dynamic masses and the ordered gravity of plans and themes.

The architecture of Aquitaine is evoked by the church of S Tomaso at Almenno San Bartolomeo in the province of Bergamo with its buttressing columns, its curves and fine, regular stonework. Its roots also lie in the Roman tradition of circular mausolea, and Lombard influence is strongly apparent in the double round-headed frieze.

On the other hand, the noble purity of the tradition of the Early Christian basilicas survives in the cathedral of S Pietro in the ancient Etruscan city of Tuscania. Behind the richly decorative façade stretches a vast unvaulted interior completed by a large, mysterious crypt.

The abbey church of S Maria at Portonovo is an authentically finished model of Romanesque. Its effect is based on a massive, bare interior with a robust vaulting system and ample space round the apse.

The famous walls of Monteriggioni mentioned by Dante are in direct contrast to this religious architecture. Their fourteen towers outlined against the dazzling sky offer a warlike impression.

## Germany

Romanesque art in Germany was directly descended from the Ottonian style and may be primarily distinguished by largeness of scale, the abiding hallmark of the German race, and by the complex arrangement of masses punctuated by many towers. These grandiose combinations make up for the rather severe decoration; they absorb it and cause it to be forgotten. The uniform principles of design are by no means indicative of sterility; they authorize a great variety of ingenious interpretations always endowed with the seal of grandeur and dignity.

The Benedictine abbey church of Alpirsbach is based on the traditional basilican model with a massive westwork and bears witness preeminently to the ascetic reforms of Hirsau. It was restored in 1960 and impresses by its exciting formal and linear purity, its height clearly cut by horizontal ceilings with open beams.

The Benedictine abbey church of Maria-Laach, dating from the very end of the Romanesque period, is completely different in character with its systematically rounded masses and its rhythmic succession of bays.

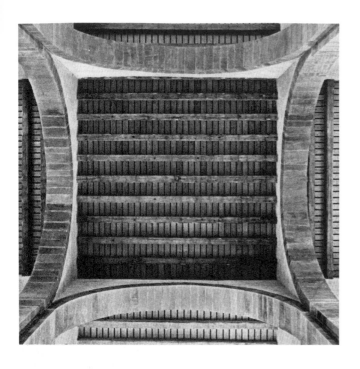

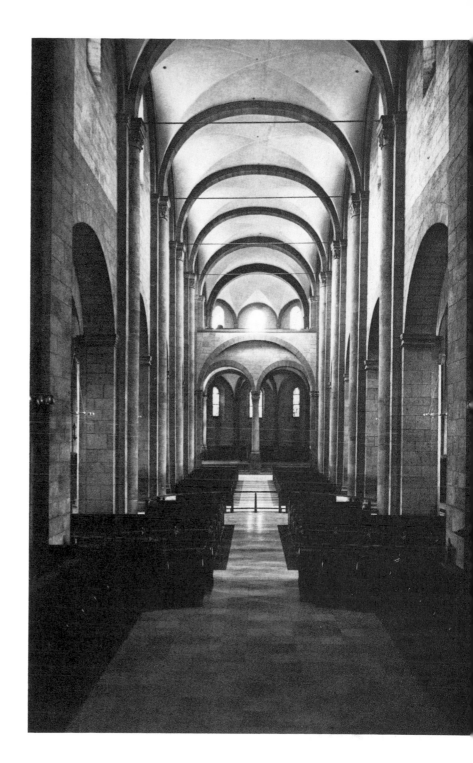

**Alpirsbach: Abbey**
Plan and longitudinal section 1:600

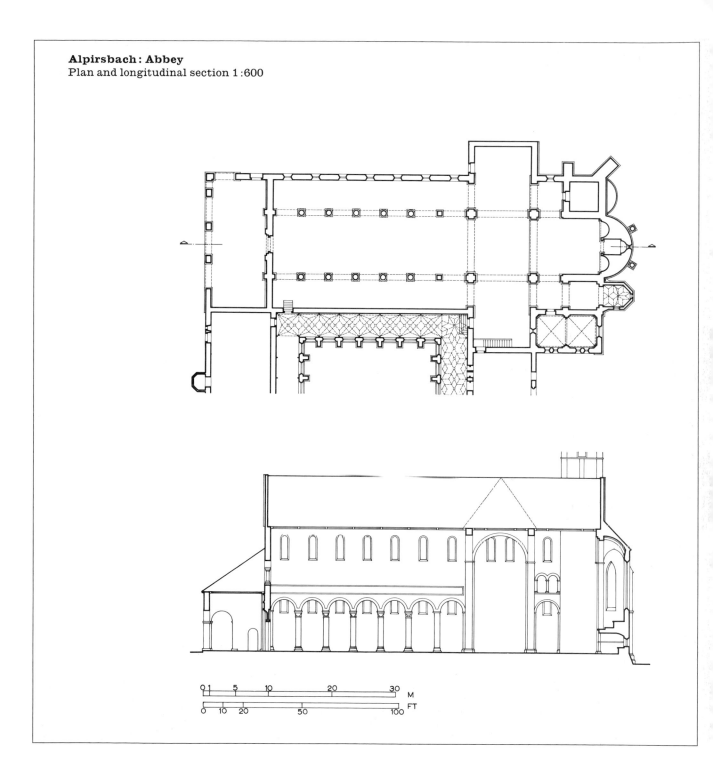

## Maria-Laach: Abbey church
Plan, elevation of chevet, longitudinal and cross sections of sanctuary 1:600

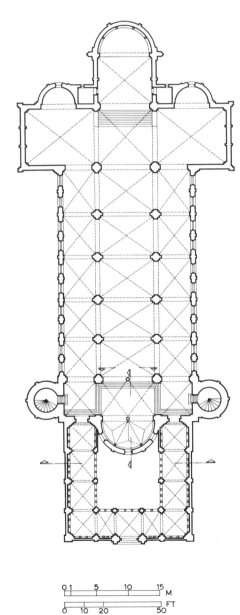

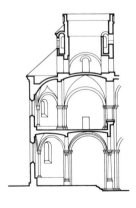

0 1    5     10      15
M

0    10    20      50
FT

# 3. Impulses and Themes

## The progress of dissemination

Were it possible to draw a map of Romanesque Europe, it would substantiate these lines of force and probably reconcile contrary impressions. From the mid-tenth to the twelfth century, conditions created centers of light brought to life by a constantly evolving civilization, side by side with areas slower to shake off the burden of anxiety and fear. Within the former there was progressive development of obscurely elaborated building techniques. Thanks to the work of patient laborers with the power of maintaining and renewing age-old inherited techniques, there resulted an authoritative, and widely disseminated style. Humanists may agree that, against this anonymous background, patrons inspired architectural prototypes capable of absorbing the flower of the available collective talent. The influence of these masterpieces continually expanded, and schools were founded whose influence sometimes spread far from their place of origin. In fact, diffusion was two-fold. Each center radiated influence outwards. Its sphere was primarily determined by conditions and organization of labor, the availability of workshops, the demand for tenders, and ways of life and tastes shared and still sensed in territories throughout Europe. Yet neighboring centers brought about hybrid zones where the ripples crossed and mingled in a disordered fashion which for a long time upset the classification of the Romanesque schools.

Thus, the Limousin is constricted between Poitou, Aquitaine and Auvergne, and the Nivernais between Auvergne and Burgundy. It also happended that more extended specialization in the workshops, a piece of good luck for the builders of poor regions, or a taste for adventure indulged by the laborers resulted in more extensive migrations which outran neighboring influences and were unaware of frontiers. Finally, the instinctive desire to imitate, subject to forms of transmission which were often accidental or unexpected, resulted in replicas and disguised reminiscences sometimes far removed from the actual model. Thus, similarities have been noted between the choir of the church at La Charité-sur-Loire and that of the church of St Omer at Lillers in Picardy, between Notre-Dame-la-Grande at Poitiers and the Schottenkirche at Regensburg, and between the architecture in the Velay and the Sacra di San Michele in Piedmont. Such affinities must be due to quite different causes. These were the usual processes regarding dissemination of influences and recreations or architectural forms, and they give rise to some kind of theory. It remains to check them and decide their local characteristics over the two centuries of the Romanesque period from the crucial years of the 950's to 1140 when the first stone of the choir of St Denis was laid.

## The Ottonian center

At the time when the West began the slow process of recovery which was to result in feudal Europe, the only civilized power endowed with influence and prestige was the Ottonian Empire. Following the death of Louis l'Enfant, the last of the Carolingians, which coincided with the establishment of the Normans on the Lower Seine, the German nobles elected Conrad the Salian their king, When he died in 936, he was replaced by his Saxon cousin, Henry the Fowler who beat the Hungarians and conquered Lorraine. This so strengthened his power that, before he died, he was able to insist on the election of his son Otto as his successor. The young king immediately clarified his political designs and ambitions by arranging his coronation to take place at Aachen, the burial place of Charlemagne. Victor over the Hungarians, laden with glory, the arbiter and light of Europe, he received the imperial crown in Rome in 962. Before he died, he arranged that the succession should pass to his son, Otto II, who effectively maintained the brilliance of the imperial court until his premature death in 983. The reign of his son, Otto III, with his grandiose ambitions, represented a unique period fostered by this continuous pattern.

The Ottonians did not limit their actions to defence of their Empire. Otto II was a cultured man, married to the discerning daughter of the Byzantine Emperor, and, like his father, planned to enhance his reign by patronage of the arts. This so-called Renaissance was further developed and strengthened by Otto III; it included architecture based on the consistent Carolingian formula of an unvaulted basilica with a massive porch at the west end of the nave, but to this were added original features.

## Development of transepts

Special efforts were brought to bear on transepts, basic elements of an architectural composition. The German architects returned to the principle of a continuous limb forming a barrier to the nave and separating it from the apse, as the Early Christian architects had already done in old St Peter's in Rome. At the abbey church of Hersfeld, the builders achieved outstanding effects by these means.

The lower transept inherited from pre-Romanesque architecture is completely different in character and scale. In these buildings the long rectangle of the basilican nave stretches unbroken from the west end to the choir. Inside, an arch only a little wider and higher than those of the aisles marks the junction of the nave with each arm of the transepts. These seem to be separated from one another by the passage of the nave and are symmetrically grouped to either side of it; they are also lower, so that the exterior is somewhat disconnected and the articulation of the building appears dry and severe.

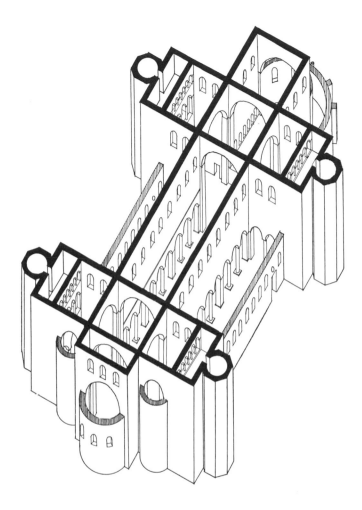

Hildesheim, Germany : St Michael. Analytical section.

A new system, known as a regular crossing, appears in the abbey church of St Michael at Hildesheim which was built from about 1015 to 1033 under the enlightened direction of Bishop Bernward, tutor of Otto III. This consists of a harmonious cruciform plan with nave and transepts of the same height meeting in a narrow crossing reduced to a square by four fine arches of equal dimensions. This plan calls for the erection of a lantern-tower which corrects the austerity of the exterior silhouette and balances the massive parallel composition at the west end also provided with a similar crossing, end turrets and apses.

## 'Composition of masses'

The Ottonian architects, motivated by design rather than conservatism, broke away from the restrictions imposed by a vaulting system and the accompanying problems of balance and distribution of thrusts, contenting themselves with the simplest designs for the naves of their churches. These were separated from the side aisles merely by semi-circular arches, carried on round or square pillars which often moved in a regular rhythm of one 'strong' pillar between two 'weak' ones. Above, there was a row of windows set in the bare wall unrelieved by any form of molding, nor was there any attempt to make them correspond to the lights at ground level. Such economy allowed the builders to realise large-scale combinations of right-angled masses which cut across one another or fitted together like a game played with gigantic cubes. At Speyer Cathedral, one of the most significant buildings of this great period, the tower over the crossing of the east transept is octagonal and completed by an arrangement of two square turrets alongside the sanctuary to the east of the wide, projecting transept arms. At one time there was a similar design at the west end where the massive entrance front took the form of a powerful transept with another octagon over the crossing and two similar turrets. The Cathedral at Trier, a typical Ottonian composition, gives a similar impression of arresting power. A semi-circular apse projects like a prow from the massive façade in which are inserted two rows of galleries with roundheaded arches; the transept arms are surmounted by two sturdy towers, extended on the west by two circular staircase turrets which project from the fabric.

## Prelude to the Romanesque

Ottonian architecture continued long after 1000; it opened the way to Romanesque art and endowed it with its accomplished maturity at a time when difficulties with papal authority coupled with internal crises in Germany itself, began to threaten Otto III. This transition was so gradual and imperceptible that German archeologists cannot agree on a definite date: some suggest 1020, others the end of the century. It may be preferable to share Louis Grodecki's opinion that this northern imperial architecture undoubtedly provided the Romanesque, which began to take hold of Western Europe about 1050, with patterns for monumental buildings with huge, spacious interiors and complex designs garnished with symmetrically placed towers: it also furnished basic elements such as regular crossings, interior galleries and alternation of supports.

About 1025 came the first use of pilasterstrips and blind arcades to bring expanses of wall to life; they are known to archeologists by the somewhat equivocal term of Lombard bands. This device was frequently varied by the use of superimposed arcades or continuous friezes extending to the level of the roof, and sometimes the effect was modified by the use of half columns in place of pilasters, or galleries hollowed out of thick apse walls.

Other discoveries, reflecting the fertile invention of the eleventh century, revived and enlarged the balanced proportions of the vast imperial basilicas. East ends were lengthened, expanded by aisles and, in some cases, enlarged by great crypts which necessitated the raising of the choir, thus reinforcing its air of majesty. As for west ends, gradual changes led to their being elaborated into splendid, severe masses flanked by the square towers which give such an air of nobility to the Romanesque church fronts

of Normandy, at Jumièges and the abbey churches of Caen, and finally resulted in the

Speyer: Cathedral. Example of groined vault.

amazing development of the Gothic cathedral façade.

The eleventh century also saw the division of naves into bays, a device highly favored by Romanesque architects. The flexible lines of arches were superimposed on the continuous elevation resulting in a modernized structure without doing away with the essential dignity of the original building. This procedure simultaneously acted as a basic form of support. In Romanesque architecture nothing is completely gratuitous and beauty of effect is only justified in so far as it results from a technical necessity.

Towards the end of the eleventh century the use of the groined vault gained ground throughout the Romanesque world, despite its complex construction, as one of the most resistant forms of roofing. Perhaps it was the most suited to be set over buildings originally designed with a timber roof as it distributed interior thrusts to its four corners.

Groined vaults originated beyond the boundaries of the Empire; later, architects there were eager to employ them. At Speyer Cathedral, for instance, their use resulted in a fascinating effect made up of the various divisions of the building which appears to invent its own boundaries. The end of the eleventh century, however, the monastic reforms of Hirsau, strongly supported by Cluny, paved the way for Cistercian asceticism, to be so strongly developed in the German lands. The Cistercian sphere of influence included 130 monasteries where a régime of strict mortification coupled with continual religious services was practised under the firm authority of their abbots. This produced a different type of architecture from that of Cluny and the German cathedrals, defined by a return to the basilican type church with a flat ceiling, and the simple masses of Early Christian architecture.

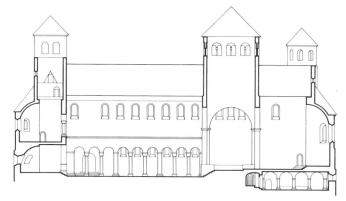

Merseburg, Germany: Cathedral. Reconstructed longitudinal section.

Thus, under cover of the Carolingian heritage, Ottonian and later, Romanesque, art in Germany witnessed a vitality which archeologists have for some time been attempting to explain more clearly. Several centers developed within the central area, varying the uniform pattern. The Cathedral of Merseburg in Saxony, the cradle of the Ottonians, is a mature example of a basilican plan church with a regular crossing and a façade showing original features, Its decoration is simple and severe, a typical characteristic of German Romanesque, unlike the sensitive sculptures produced by contemporary craftsmen in Burgundy, Aquitaine, Auvergne and Provence. The lands of the Meuse favored low transepts, massive west ends dominated by a single tower and giant orders set in motion by wall arcades with roundheaded arches. With the succession of the Franconian dynasty which replaced the Ottonians after 1024, the region of the Middle Rhine took architectural precedence over other districts, the cathedrals of Trier, Speyer, Mainz and Worms being the finest of its great buildings. Finally, after the second quarter of the eleventh century, the commercial centers of the Lower Rhine — Cologne, Aachen, Utrecht and Essen, embarked on fresh innovations which included subtle decorative work.

## Beyond the frontiers of the Empire

The authoritative influence of the Ottonian style, prolonged by the contribution of the Romanesque, made itself felt far beyond the frontiers of the Empire. Endowed with prodigious powers of expansion, it enveloped the entire region set in an arc round the western boundaries, stretching from the Scandinavian countries to Normandy. We may even feel obliged to reject eleventh-century political setting in favor of a classification based on stylistic analysis, grouping in a single block all the so-called regional styles from the Atlantic to the Elbe, and from the North Sea to the Alps and the Loire.

The Romanesque builders of the eleventh century had some magnificent protoypes available in the form of some important Benedictine abbeys in eastern and north-eastern France, the last stronghold of the Carolingians. They included St Riquier with its twin symmetrical transepts and its two rounded, staged towers, St Denis, and several others. Throughout the eleventh century these models were used as a base for experiments concerning the hollowing out of the heavy, almost solid, walls separating naves from aisles. The cathedral of Tournai serves as a final example, at a time when the Gothic style was coming into being elsewhere. This famous church was rebuilt after 1110, consecrated in 1171, and provided in the thirteenth century with a fine ogival choir — rather out of keeping with the Romanesque nave and transepts. A rare feature of its plan are rounded transept arms with ambulatories and galleries whose functions appear to be architectural rather than liturgical. It was a question of lightening the walls by hollowing them out in several layers.

The elevation of the nave of ten bays resembles a Roman aqueduct on account of its four imposing storeys with their echoes of the antique. Firmly indicated lines stress the courses: low, rounded arches exactly surmounted by those of the triforium, then a reduced arcade framing small round-headed bays topped by a row of clerestory windows behind which runs an exterior wall-passage. Gaps and masses blend in noble harmony. The shadowy recesses of the two lower storeys are mysteriously illuminated by light filtered through the windows of the aisles and galleries, forming a striking contrast to the direct lighting of the upper bays and accentuating the stiffness of the horizontal design. The bays are not stressed by any vertical supports: these are merely discreetly hinted at by the super-imposed arches.

St Benoît-sur-Loire: Abbey church (left). Caen: St Etienne (right). Elevations.

## Normandy and England

Of all the provinces possessing buildings showing the delayed influence of Carolingian architecture, Normandy achieved exceptional results in applying the harmonious combination of the principles of horizontality and verticality which was possibly the key experience of the Romanesque. The Normans reaped the benefits of demographic prosperity and a vitality to which the activities of their mercenaries bear witness. Emigrating to the service of the Dukes of Lombardy, they ended by setting up enclaves on Italian soil and acting as equivocal defenders of the Holy See. In Normandy itself the question of the succession of Robert the Devil who died in 1035, leaving only one bastard son, William, gave rise to a formidable crisis. The coalition formed against the young heir was finally broken up when he routed the royalist army at Mortemer in 1054. Twelve years later, having consolidated his prestige, he crossed the Channel, disembarked in England, and, in the course of a single day, won a resounding victory over the Saxon King Harold.

In England, there was no resistance to the Conqueror. Moreover, he had at his command the valuable cooperation of the Church, and particularly the Norman monks. Normandy itself was rich in great and famous abbeys including St Wandrille, Jumièges, Fécamp, St Georges de Boscherville, Le Bec-Hellouin which was a center of international culture, and the Abbaye-aux-Hommes and Abbaye-aux-Dames at Caen founded by Duke William himself. From Le Bec-Hellouin came Lanfranc of Milan who was appointed the first abbot of the Abbaye-aux-Hommes thanks to William's favor, and later, in 1070, became Archbishop of Canterbury and Primate of England. The influence of such men extended building activity which had begun in the first half of the century with the erection of the churches of Bernay where William of Volpiano had been abbot, Mont-Saint-Michel and Jumièges. The Benedictines of Mont-Saint-Michel rebuilt their church on the summit of its storm beaten rock after 1022-3. The elevation of the nave was typically tripartite: great round-headed arches, without alternation of supports, set on square pillars with imbedded columns, a triforium with twin bays compressed below deep surrounding archivolts, and clerestory windows. The division into bays is emphasized by the pronounced embedded columns of the nave which rise the whole height of the walls to receive the trusses of the timber vault. At Jumièges, on the other hand, there was strict alternation in the nave which was rebuilt between 1052 and 1067. Alternate strong piers were reinforced on the nave side by massive half-columns embedded in the pilasters; these half-columns strengthened the inner wall to the level of the upper windows. The interiors of the two abbeys at Caen strongly resemble one another. At the Abbaye-aux-Hommes, a system of alternation is suggested by the careful accentuation of the vertical feature strengthening the wall, but allowing free expansion to the lines of heavy horizontal arches at ground level and in the galleries above. The effect must have been even more imposing before the addition of a rib vault, when the clerestory lightening the upper wall still provided an authoritative conclusion to the tripartite elevation.

This severity of design may still be admired unaltered in the naves of several English Romanesque churches built under Norman influence after the Conquest. The nave of Binham Priory in Norfolk, which lacks alternation, is cut short by a horizontal ceiling and so are those at Romsey, Selby and Waltham abbeys. The alternated naves of these three churches are powerfully articulated with arcaded galleries and wall-passages. It has often been noted that this system with the sturdy rhythm of its great pillars and its vertical scansion must have been a predestined foundation for rib vaults; in fact, the Norman architects, after obstinately refusing to vault the naves of their major churches, suddenly decided to roof the choir of Durham Cathedral with a rib vault, after which this new device was freely used. It is necessary, however, to recognize that the adoption of transepts completely upset the austere arrangement of the older churches and obscured the specific function of their high walls which was to act as supports for the timber roofing, like the two raised arms of an Atlas.

## The Architects of Como

In the shelter of the Alps north of Milan, the masons of Como, the 'maestri comacini' devoted themselves, on the other hand, to early experiments with vaulting. Italian archeologists have thrown considerable light on their individual activity — one's interest is heightened by the beautiful mountainous background against which they worked. Their activity developed against a background of virtual historical chaos. At Byzantium, from 568 onwards, the barbarian invaders who had overthrown the Empire of the West were contending for the remnants of the Italian peninsula while, simultaneously, the Lombards from Germany were settling in Northern Italy and were also threatening the papal territories by founding the principalities of Benevento, Capua and Salerno. The Arabs gained a foothold in Southern Italy and Hungarian invaders added still further to the confusion. The leadership of Rome had fallen into the hands of weak, shadowy or criminal Popes and had ceased to be of any account. This general state of anarchy favored the ambitions of Otto I which reached their peak of fullfilment with his coronation at Rome in 962.

Some small islands of refuge continued stubbornly and precariously to foster the artistic tradition of the Empire. They included a few

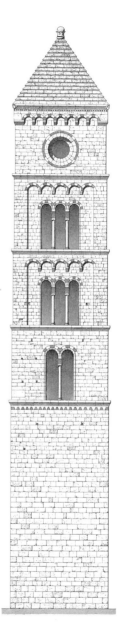

Uzès: Church. Circular bell-tower (Tour Fenestrelle).

Puissalicon: Church. Square bell-tower.

134

monasteries and two tiny islands, the Isola Comacina in Lake Como and the Isola S Giulio in Lake Orta. Here was reborn a civilization based on stone, and a practical, comparatively rapid technique of building. This was defined by the use of rough, local materials broken up by means of hammers, and then fashioned into small elongated strips merely supplemented by tufa or round pebbles from the streams in mountain districts where there were few quarries; by the balance demanded by the piling up of stone rather than by its skilful placing; and by the use of heavy piers to support the rough masonry. Both interiors and exteriors were austere and crudely executed, though the interior plaster facings could accomodate dramatic wall paintings similar to those found in some remote churches in Catalonia and Roussillon. Diaphragm arches set across the width of the nave heralded the division into bays characteristic of later Romanesque architecture, and broke the monotony of the basilican design.

Outside, extraordinary bell-towers and campaniles rose above the squat buildings. These towers were usually square, but sometimes round or octagonal when over a transept crossing, with superimposed twin-bayed apertures on each of their slim sides. They were not so much the work of skilled architects as of patient artisans disciplined by much practice in imitation, the transmission of professional methods, and the ability to find solutions to suit any situation.

There was no form of sculptured decoration. Interior supports were topped by plain imposts or projecting cushions to receive the springs of the arches, or by unadorned capitals in the shape of a cube with their lower portions rounded off, for which reason they are known as block capitals. Exteriors were sometimes ornamented with a rough tracery of herring-bone work, or indented moldings, or by the insertion

of a layer of large stones which helped to give cohesion to the structure. The keynote of the system, however, was the animation of walls by a rhythm of alternate projecting bands and hollow, rectangular panels, their upper portions scalloped into little carved arches grouped either in twos and threes or in a series. This form of decoration, erroneously known as 'Lombard bands,' glides along the walls of apses, naves and façades and flows over the exteriors of bell-towers, shimmering in the sunlight of Mediterranean countries. They are also hollowed out in the exterior walls of apses where they develop into a series of niches: these are the origin of the beautiful galleries or 'loggie' which encircle the chevets of Romanesque churches in Southern Europe, and were enthusiastically adopted by German builders.

The progressive stabilization of the tenth century soon increased the field of influence of these local craftsmen, and introduced them to the new workshops of Europe. Their emigration is a striking phenomenon on account of its scope and the mystery surrounding its methods, and forms one of the richest and most exciting chapters in the story of Romanesque development.

## Catalonia

This economy of means and ease of adaptation to all types and designs of buildings was highly attractive. Once again, however, logical developments are upset by historical fact. The most natural thing would have been for the comacine style to spread from its center of origin by the nearest routes over the Alps. Yet, strangely enough, the first foreign province to make use of it, in the mid-tenth century, was Catalonia, separated from the Italian lakes by the sea and by Provence, then being ravaged by the Saracens. Charlemagne had made Catalonia into a stable frontier region able to withstand Arab pressures and to maintain its independence; since his time, it had remained a window to the Mediterranean world.

The only reference to comacine craftsmen in Catalonian documents is late in date: a contract of 1175, drawn up for the completion of the cathedral of Urgel, includes four 'Lombards' and their associates. There is little doubt, however, that these influences penetrated to Catalonia very early on. From the late tenth century onwards, they swarmed over the province, rejuvenating and transforming the ancient native traditions based on Mozarabic architectural styles. These conclusions, however, would be more definite if they could be confirmed by textual references.

None of the explanations provided by archeologists are sufficiently conclusive. It is better to agree to the simpler explanation that the introduction of comacine forms was due to a conjunction of opportune circumstances: the economic awaking and repopulation of central Catalonia favored by the simultaneous weakening and collapse of the caliphate of Córdoba, and the availability of bands of adventurous craftsmen from abroad who offered their services, and were delighted to find the familiar fine, colored limestone which was so suited to their work. However this may be, the innovation had happy results. It offered the Roman liturgy which had, after some difficulties, replaced the Mozarabic form, wide, spacious apses. Various circular and trefoil plans were adopted, but it was more usual to design a basilican type building dominated by a transept with a dome over the crossing. Moreover, the Catalans had many fine quarries and devoted themselves to providing the naves of their churches with stone vaults from an early date. The first example quoted is the nave of the church of Bañolas which was consecrated in 888, burned by Arabs, and rebuilt in stone in 957.

This diffusion of comacine techniques continued to expand after the beginning of the eleventh century. It reduced, but did not put an end to the traditional ornamental sculpture inspired by Arab art, nor did it bring about the closure of the workshops of the Pyrenean marble-cutters who continued to export their products (particularly carved altar tables). Elsewhere, early anonymity gives way to documented work, including the plans adopted by Abbot Oliba for his monasteries at Ripoll and St Michel de Cuxa and his cathedral at Vich. The majestic dignity of these buildings was enhanced by their complex design and by monumental bell-towers which were the pride of early Romanesque art in the South.

## The spread of the Mediterranean forms of early Romanesque art

These impulses profited to the full from the social and economic revival following the tenth century. The new forms broke out from Catalonia in two directions. With progress south blocked by the Arabs, they traveled across the valleys of the eastern Pyrenees to Andorra and Aragon. Further north the Catalan style triumphed in the Cerdagne and Roussillon, now reunited under the same crown. It also penetrated the 'garrigues' as far as the Cévennes; its influence was welcomed along the coast of Languedoc and in the liberated territories of Provence. In the northern tip of this area, the exterior of the church of Cruas, one of the most important in the valley of the Middle Rhône, is possibly influenced by a distant memory of an Ottonian plan. Nevertheless, its general interior and exterior arrangement plainly indicates southern influences.

The progress of these influences northwards along the corridor of the Rhône came to a halt in the region of Vienne and Lyons due to conservatism inherited from the Roman imperial tradition.

The distant influence of Catalonia stretched beyond the Alpes Maritimes to link up with the continued propagation of ideas by the comacine architects. The influence of Como stretched across the Lombard plain and made itself felt as far as Liguria and Tuscany where, shortly after 1200, it inspired fine, heavily ornamented, gabled façades with rows of pillared arcades. Dalmatia, too, came within their sphere of influence. In these regions, however, they suffered from the competition of Byzantine styles and craftsmen: for instance, the grandiose plan for the cathedral at Pisa begun in 1063 was the creation of a Greek named Basketos. The architects of Como then crossed their native Alps, and by way of the Engadine, reached Tyrol and the Grisons. Over the St Gothard and the Simplon, they gained the roads leading across the Swiss plateau to the abbeys and busy cities of the Rhine. In the west, they passed through the Val d'Aosta and the deep valleys cutting through the Piedmontese Alps, and, crossing the Great St Bernard, they expanded over the Valais where they restored the abbey church of Agaune. St Odilo rebuilt the Cluniac priories of Payerne and Romainmôtier under the influence of their techniques which extended even further to the plateaux of the Jura. Here they became so well established that, in many cases, the first rib vaults were set on structures that had remained Lombard in style with heavy, irregularly alternating pillars and exterior facings of blind arcades.

## From Burgundy to Provence

It is possible that eleventh century Burgundy owed its special position in the geography of early Romanesque art to similar forms of transmission, in which roads seem to have had a predominant part. Situated at the crossroads of routes from the Rhône and the Jura and continually experiencing the events of history, the province was well placed geographically to receive the Mediterranean styles which it could have adapted and developed in accordance with its individual genius. This, however, would suggest that the province had more than its real share of traffic, which, in actual fact, seems to have passed further north by way of Besançon and Alsace.

History has, in this case, left sufficient clues for us to be able to unravel the web of this sudden penetration. The energetic William of Volpiano was responsible for the comacine style (that of his native land), being introduced to Dijon at St Bénigne. We may also suppose that it was simultaneously brought to Tournus by his friend, Abbot Wago, who was also well-known at St Bénigne. Further west it scarcely penetrated the regions between the Saône and the Loire. In the country round Mâcon and Chalon-sur-Saône, however, it was taken up and developed by the local masons in the eleventh century and given an immense support by St Hugh's Cluny; its influence was so deep and lasting that buildings continued to reflect it even as late as the twelfth century, despite appreciable stylistic developments. In Provence it was not so obvious; here the authority of early Mediterranean Romanesque had to blend with memories of Roman architecture whose noble ruins provided countless models and examples. Thus, it made up for the architectural void which existed on either side of the Rhône valley between the spheres of influence of Ottonian architecture and the styles which flourished further west in Aquitaine.

## The Centers of Aquitaine

This portion of Europe formed a completely different world, an almost individual civilization that had not been upset or influenced by the Empire or the diffusion of Mediterranean customs. Since the time of the Roman Empire a feeling of national unity seems to have persisted in Aquitaine. Odo of Touraine, the future Abbot of Cluny, spent much of his youth at the court of Aquitaine where he was an intimate of the Count of Anjou. Geographically, the province of Aquitaine included two very different regions: the greater part of the uplands of Central France from their eastern slopes to the hills of the Limousin, and, spread round them in a semi-circle, the fertile districts of Poitou, Saintonge and Angoumois. In the eleventh century these regions were filled with Romanesque churches whose original and diverse features could not conceal, on closer examination, the persistent family likeness which formed a link between them, the result of their shared origin. They probably responded freely to the influence of Moslem art which was transmitted to them from Christian Spain over the passes of the Pyrenees. From it they inherited, among other features, an original type of cusped arch frequently found in Auvergne.

With the end of the Norman invasions, building activity was resumed in Touraine and the Loire valley, and the results, or their remains may be seen to herald the advent of the Romanesque style. Work was evidently conducted on a methodical basis: large, regular blocks for the chief portions of the fabric, small stones or rubble for surface dressing, combinations of inlay and imaginative color inherited from antique, pre-Romanesque tradition. Pillars were broken down into engaged half-columns, each element assuming a rational function of support. Articulation was created by the arrangement and intersection of lines and plane surfaces. Arches were fully rounded, and exterior shapes and buttresses cleverly camouflaged by columns. There were some purely decorative features, chief of which were the sculptured corbels, frequently used in the eleventh century over an area extending as far as Nivernais and Brionnais, and there were early attempts at anthropomorphic sculpture. All these points were

mastered by the new style. Other examples show that neighboring provinces were also subject to these influences whose freedom of invention did not suffer from submission to strict standardization as was the case with Lombard art. Civaux and St Pierre-les-Eglises are representative of Poitou, and the tenth century buildings of Auvergne also bear witness to this theory.

## Auvergne

The ancient territory of the Arverni seems to have played the part of a defensive stronghold in the high Middle Ages. The inhabitants of the mountains, protected by their natural ramparts, watched the barbarian raiders laying waste the plains below them. On the heights they were accustomed to the roughest weathers, were quick to practise evasion, and lived and worked as best they could. Lack of information prevents us from examining their life, but there are a few indications which provide us with some clues. Since the opening centuries of the Christian era, the shrine of the Virgin at Le Puy had been visited by the sick wishing to be cured, and, in 957, Bishop Godescalc undertook the hazardous pilgrimage to Compostela. He ordered an oratory to be built in honor of the Archangel Michael on the summit of the precipitous cone of the Aiguilhe. Later, in 992, the Pope, with complete disregard for the approach of the millennium, founded a jubilee for Le Puy which was to be celebrated whenever Good Friday coincided with the feast of the Annunciation. The windswept heights were dominated by the ancient Abbey of St Chaffre famous for the martyrdom of its second abbot, Theofred, by the Saracens. Godescalc was abbot here in the mid-tenth century, so that the destinies of Auvergne were virtually in the hands of one strong man.

The Bishop of Auvergne at this period was the great Stephen II who summoned the Cluniacs to the priory of Sauxillanges where Peter the Venerable was later to be a humble monk. He rebuilt the cathedral at Clermont-Ferrand, and its splendor was known throughout the land. This is sure proof that the masons and decorators of Auvergne were capable, even in these difficult times, of creating an impressive masterpiece. Stephen also commissioned a magnificent gold figure of the Virgin in majesty from his clerk, Aléaume, to enclose the cathedral relics; this was the prototype, according to Louis Bréhier, of all the others venerated in Auvergne. Aléaume also executed the awesome effigy of Ste Foy, the crumbling, bejeweled figure which dominates the treasury at Conques.

Despite some exaggeration, Stephen II's cathedral, the prototype of so many fine churches, probably justified the admiration accorded it. As far as can be made out from a fairly vague, allegorical description, it combined some Early Christian features, including an atrium, with completely new elements such as a western narthex with a gallery and a chevet with no fewer than a dozen chapels set around the apse. A crypt which was discovered in the nineteenth century contained an ambulatory round which were set two, if not three, radiating chapels of rectangular plan. This was the first

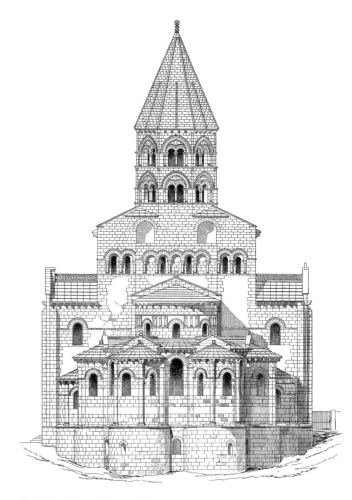

Orcival: Notre-Dame du Port. Oblong central feature.

Clermont-Ferrand: Notre-Dame du Port. Side view.

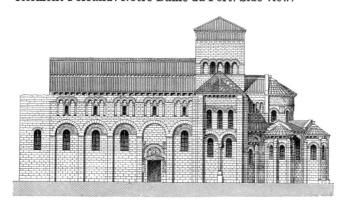

rough and untried example of a program that was to undergo considerable development during the Romanesque period. There is reason to believe that it was immediately adopted at St Maurice d'Agaune in the Valais, a basilica which was destroyed by the Saracens and was still a ruin when St Odo saw it in 941. It is also possible that it was adopted in the tenth century for the crypt of the abbey church at Tournus.

It is not known whether the chevet of Stephen

139

II's cathedral at Clermont reproduced the plan of the crypt. Despite the early examples at Agaune and, possibly, Tournus, the formula of an ambulatory with radiating chapels is rarely found in the region near the Rhône which remained loyal to the pre-Romanesque tradition of staggered apses often embedded in massive walls; Romanesque influence is only apparent at Valence cathedral and St Gilles-du-Gard. On the other hand, the beauty of the interior and exterior of Clermont, the suitability of its design to the veneration of relics and the movements of crowds of worshippers, and the increasing study of its elevations assured it a wide distribution over the extreme west of Europe, from St Etienne at Nevers and St Benoît-sur-Loire to the cathedral of Santiago. The design was also taken up by the builders of the great abbey church at Cluny and by the architects of Paray-le-Monial, La Charité-sur-Loire and Notre-Dame at Beaune. It was also reproduced about 1006 at the new basilica built over the tomb of St Martin at Tours, and again a few years later, at the church of St Aignan in Orléans (if we may trust the evidence of the chronicler Helgaud). In the actual district of Clermont, it was incorporated in a magnificent series of buildings which expressed one of the most perfect syntheses achieved by the Romanesque.

Probably in order to avoid pronounced sagging of the nave vault which was built of heavy materials and had no ribs, the Clermont architects buttressed it with aisles surmounted by spacious galleries with quadrant vaults and a fine line of arches opening into the main nave. The lofty dome on squinches, above which was an octagonal belfry, was balanced by two collateral bays which extended the aisles and were also quadrant-vaulted: these helped to ease the transition to the lower transepts. This typical massive, oblong layout varied little, whether at Notre-Dame-du-Port, Orcival, St Nectaire, St Austremoine at Issoire or St Saturnin. West of the nave was a narthex and, past the apsidal dome supported by raised columns and surrounded by an ambulatory, the choir descends to the lower radiating apses. Regular, widely joined masonry and a combination of painted woodwork with blind wall arcades completed the bold outlines of these buildings set against their strange background of extinct volcanoes. The churches of the pilgrimage roads which can hardly be fitted into an individual school merely added transept aisles to this formula, a logical conclusion to the system. Nevertheless they did not have a monopoly in this, as the same plan was adopted for the new cathedral at Pisa.

## Western France

The Atlantic shore and its hinterland stretching from the mouth of the Loire to the headlands of Galicia was more than the route taken by pilgrims in the eleventh and twelfth centuries on their march to Santiago. It was also the setting for centers of civilization which bordered on one another and exchanged influences. Here, perhaps, beat the real heart of Romanesque art; in these vital regions, inventive craftsmen produced many of its liveliest, most typical creations in an atmosphere of complete freedom. Neither the stultifying conformity of Carolingian and Ottonian survivals which did not admit the support of sculpture incorporated in a building to heighten its effect until a very late date, nor the rustic laws of early Mediterranean Romanesque art prevented the flowering of structural decoration in full association with the architecture.

Poitou probably came at the head of the list. The art of building flourished here from an early date. In the early eleventh century, the Countess of Poitou restored the monastery of Ligugé, famous for its associations with St. Martin, and also founded Maillezais, which almost immediately achieved a lasting reputation. 1049 witnessed the consecration of the pilgrimage shrine of St Hilaire at Poitiers which was supported by another member of the house of Aquitaine – Emma, cousin of Duke William and Queen of England. William himself was an ardent pilgrim and paid annual visits to Rome or Santiago. He also threw open his duchy to Cluniac influence. In the late eleventh century the town of Poitiers had its full share of magnificent buildings and became the center of an original type of cultural life. Duke William IX of Aquitaine was known as the first of the troubadours, and this rich civilization took its tone from his work.

There was also great activity in the sphere of building; interiors were covered in amazing frescoes. The abundant variety of the Romanesque architecture of Poitou possesses an airy lightness emphasized by the quality of the colored limestone used. Naves are completely vaulted and buttressed by high, narrow aisles which are the only source of light. Slender pillars support great rounded arches and stress the elevation of the interior with their soaring height. Round columns of basilican type stand next to slim, four-lobed supports. Chevets expand into ambulatories and radiating chapels. Exterior silhouettes make varied use of colonnades, one of the most typical examples being the famous belfry of St Porchaire at Poitiers. Large-scale, three-storeyed façades are sometimes covered with a riot of ornament which miraculously never becomes overloaded. Probably, the reason for this is the absence of tympana, the opening up of a large bay beneath the gable and a skilful allocation of undecorated spaces which allow sufficient points of repose. In short, this is an eclectic art making use of all the attractive features in the repertory with an assured taste.

Angoumois, Saintonge, Périgord and Quercy participated to varying degrees in this rich flowering. Girard de Blaye, Bishop of Angoulême did not limit his patronage to the rebuilding of his cathedral; a Norman by birth and a papal legate, he made his diocese into a lively art center. Besides the adoption of the system of a series of domes for his cathedral, we owe to him the dissemination of a type of façade where blind wall arcades form unexpected projections, thus giving an impressively monumental effect. Like many other Romanesque forms, this system sprang from a tentative discovery first made by artisans. This was later grasped by a talented architect and expanded into a synthesis which was set up as a model and inspiration for an entire generation. At the abbey church of Cellefrouin, it appears as no more than a noble rhythm of six lofty blind arcades backed by a plain front punctuated by four supporting columns like organ pipes. The achievement of Bishop Girard and the builders of the front of Angoulême cathedral was the heightening of the middle arch so as to enclose both the door and the window above it, the insertion of a blind arcade with sculptured tympana above each of the side arches at ground level, and filling the entire portion of the front below the gable and the towers with six smaller, more delicate wall arcades. The dislike of empty spaces common to Romanesque architects was alleviated by the areas of relaxation offered by the bare expanses of wall below the central tympanum and the large arcades at each end. This was the system which was later so successfully used in church façades in the Charente in the twelfth century.

The decoration of all these fronts is extremely plain, with horizontal lines proclaimed either by a continuous single gallery as at La Couronne, Dirac and Moulidars, or by two superimposed galleries of different lengths, such as add to the quiet dignity of the façades of Gensac-La-Pallue and Châtres. On the other hand, the exteriors of the Romanesque churches of Saintonge are typified by exuberant ornament that sometimes renders them stiff. Wild compositions full of imaginary beasts and monsters are set against delicately hewn stone backgrounds and carved scallops.

The contrasting severity of the domed churches of Périgord with their bare façades may have been due to their proximity to the wild, hilly regions. This seems doubtful, however, considering that the plateaux of Quercy, which are just as much linked to the regions of the Center geographically and historically, were widely influenced by the revival of monumental statuary. The simultaneous influence of Islam also makes its presence felt at Oloron. The transept of the church of the Holy Cross in the upper town is roofed by a dome with crossed ribs, deriving directly from those of the mosque at Córdoba.

## Atlantic Spain

Christian Spain, both north and west, also testified to the part played by the great pilgrimage to Compostela and its inspired craftsmen in the diffusion of Romanesque art. It fell to Alfonso VI, friend of St Hugh of Cluny, to build roads, bridges and hospices, that made the route to Santiago into a national artery the Cluniacs reformed and founded monasteries, but had no influence over architectural development in Castile, León or distant Galicia.

The rich, complex, still relatively unknown Spanish Romanesque gives signs of many other stylistic connections. Throughout the western sector of the country there was a link with the provinces of Languedoc and Aquitaine to which it was joined by the famous passes of Le Somport and Roncevaux. As in the case of the Alps, this shows that mountain ranges have seldom proved an impassable barrier, but have more often served to form a bond between the territories on either side of them, making them interdependent. The chronology of the Panteón de los Reyes, the strange rectangular building preceding the church of S Isidoro at León, may be controver-sial, but there can be no doubt of the influence of the tower-porch of St Benoît-sur-Loire on the structure. The warm tones of the many village churches resemble those of Poitou and Saintonge with their perfected stonecutting, their rounded outlines, buttressing columns, arcaded galleries and delicately carved doorways. Only the slightest hint of Arab influence is evident – at least until the later development of the Mudéjar style. At the cathedral of Santiago both the Puerta de las Platerîas at the end of the south transept and the Pórtico de la Gloria carved by Master Matthew at the west end are stunning proof that Spanish Romanesque sculpture was far from being a weak imitation of that of Languedoc. The reliefs on the four corner pillars of the famous cloisters at Silos whose carved capitals resemble ivories are more than a subtle reflection of the style of Moissac: they are powerful, original creations endowed with a strange, dreamlike charm. The panel which includes a joint representation of the 'Entombment' and the 'Resurrection' reveals itself as one of the highest achievements of Romanesque sculpture and, indeed, of all art. Within the frame of a roundheaded arch supported by two slim columns with capitals, two registers are formed by a horizontal lintel. The dead Christ rests on this and the two bearers, ranged symmetrically, bend down towards the body. On the left, an angel is in the act of raising the slab from the sepulcher so that its point rests on the abacus of the capital above. One of the bearers has seized the body's right arm which is thus in line with this vigorous sideways thrust. The women advancing to the tomb are portrayed as identical silhouettes and form three commanding verticals at the right-hand side of the panel. The guards of the tomb are grouped theatrically below the lintel. Those at each end face one another and seem to be executing a gymnastic movement on their bended knees. Five more guards, arranged fan-wise, fill the V-shaped space between their inclined bodies.

# Plates

## Ely Cathedral

147 The fine large-scale nave built c.1080-1090, an example of a Norman church with tripartite elevation and alternating supports.

148 Elevation of the nave. In contrast to the churches of the Empire, there is perfect harmony and symmetry between the three storeys of superimposed openings and a progressive reduction of masses: a single bay at ground level, two in the triforium and three in the upper clerestory. By this means the spectator's eye is led on by the attraction of light from simplicity to complexity.

149 Detail of a pillar (above).
Norman-type decorative wall arcades with interlaced arches and cushion capitals (below).

## Castle Hedingham

150 One of the huge keeps built at the time of the Conquest to ensure control of the country. The massive rectangle has four storeys, stands on a mount, and is faced in alternating panels. Square staircase turrets occupy two of the corners. There are few light openings, especially in the more vulnerable lower storeys.

151 Round-headed bay from a lower storey with a triple archivolt supported by two small columns.

## Saone (Syria): Castle

152 The ditch hollowed out of the rock showing the peculiar needle left to support a footbridge.

153 Detail of the defence system. On the left are traces of Byzantine walls built of small stones in the Roman fashion, and the square keep.

154 Rusticated doorway with a discharging arch above the lintel.

155 General view of the fortress from the east. In the foreground, the great ditch and the keep.

## Tahull (Spain)

156 **S Maria.** This church, situated in the heart of Catalonia, was consecrated in 1123; together with its sister church, S Clemente, it remains wholly loyal to the traditions of the early comacine style.

157 Detail of the apse arcade.

158 Dome over the crossing (restored).

159 The choir.

160 **S Clemente.** The Lombard campanile.

161 One of the small apses. Arcading with half-columns.

162 Elevation of the campanile with superimposed bands.

163 Paintings in the apse (now in the Barcelona Museum).

## Cardona

164 **S Vicente** in the upper town.

165 Dome on squinches over the crossing.

166 The porch.

167 Elevation of the nave.

168 Perspective through the aisle.

## Estella (Spain)

169 Romanesque house with round-headed arcades on the road to Santiago.

170 Capital of one of the buttress-columns.

**Ely : Cathedral**
Plan 1 :1000

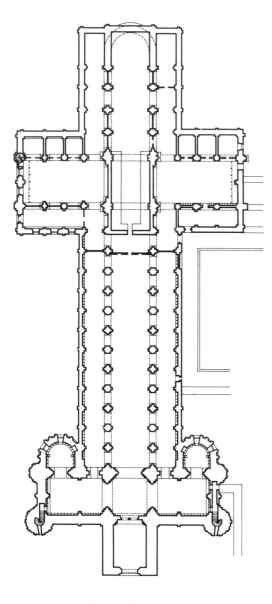

**Castle Hedingham, Essex**
Plan and section 1 :400

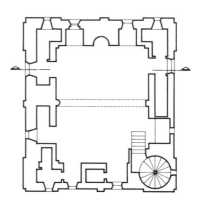

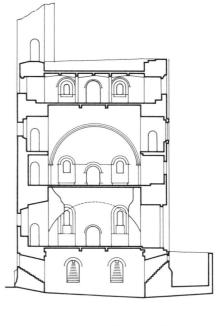

0 1 5 10 20 30 M
0 10 20 50 100 FT

0 1 5 10 15 M
0 10 20 50 FT

## Saone, Syria: Castle

Plan 1:3000. Plan of keep, section of great ditch and elevation of keep 1:600

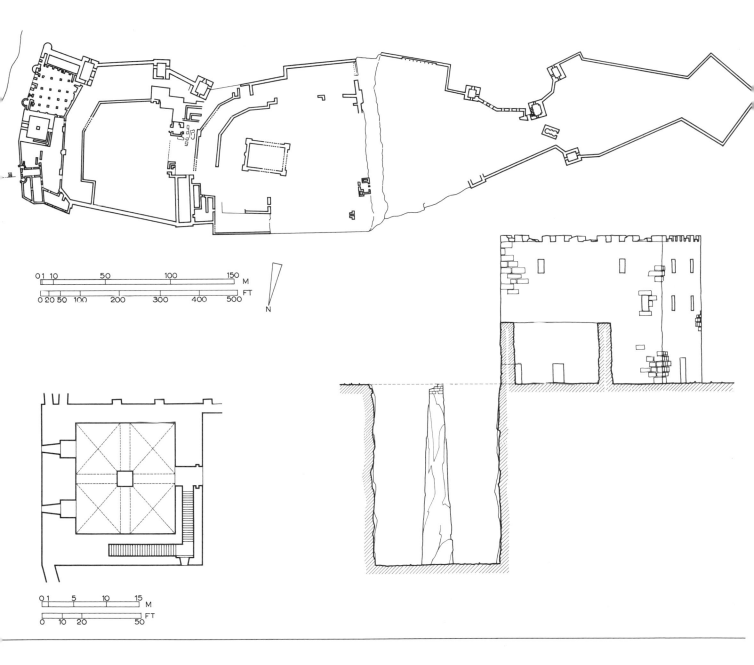

# Notes

## Great Britain

There is a basic difference between English and Continental Romanesque architecture. The English style did not arise from a spontaneous act of creation in the country itself or from the rich aspiration of instinctive genius. It was a foreign art imported from abroad, the fruit of war and the principle of conquest – in fact, of military occupation. There were few examples prior to the Norman invasion of 1066, though some rebuilding took place in the late tenth century during the work of reunion inspired by the Saxon kings, including the cathedrals of Winchester, Canterbury and Elmham. These churches reflected local inspiration but were scarcely indicative of the vast building enterprises that were to follow the Conquest. Liberally endowed with means and anxious to confirm their prestige, the Normans founded and built many large Benedictine abbeys which, under the direction of their imperious abbots, were to be one of their liveliest political instruments. Some of the finest Norman churches, easily indentifiable, arose on English soil. They share the robust proportions of Ottonian architecture and their naves display superb tripartite elevations: great arches with rich, round moldings, triforia or wide galleries, and an upper passage running above the pillars in front of clerestory windows. This system grows more and more reduced as it rises to receive the flat ceiling of the nave which abruptly terminates its height. Buildings of this type include Battle Abbey, St Augustine's Abbey at Canterbury, and the cathedrals of Winchester, Worcester, Gloucester whose round pillars recall Payerne, Norwich with its fine ambulatory, and Ely. The first rib vaults appeared at Durham cathedral at the very end of the eleventh century.

This magnificent flowering was all the more remarkable as it developed in a country that was still far from being pacified. Its new masters organized a defensive system on an impressive scale. No fewer than 1200 castles were built between 1066 and 1089, though some of them were no more than mere mounds or enclosures. They included the White Tower of the Tower of London which survives more or less unchanged and the keeps of Rochester and Hedingham.

## The Holy Land

The Crusaders had to make a similar effort in Palestine. Following the capture of the holy city of Jerusalem in 1099 and the sudden conquest of the coastal towns which were to form the basis of the Latin Kingdom, there arose a simultaneous need to build Christian sanctuaries to replace the basilicas of Constantine and the Byzantine churches, to equip badly needed ports and to defend the weak desert frontiers from the ceaseless threats of the Infidels. This last necessity was probably the most imperative. Apart from a few traces of exotic influence, the religious architecture of the East, whether at the Holy Sepulcher or the delightful church of St Anne at Nazareth, was virtually a repetition of the themes and styles of late Romanesque in the West. Some fascinating resemblances can only be explained by the migrations of artists. The fortresses guarded by the military orders, on the other hand, profited to the full from the considerable advances made by Byzantine engineers. The castles of Saone, Margat and Krak des Chevaliers, in their breathtaking positions commanding the routes usually taken by raiders and invaders, still bear powerful witness to the fleeting temporal ascendancy of the Franks over the Holy Places.

## Spain

Romanesque art in Spain, from Catalonia to Galicia, also interpreted and celebrated an epic, this time that of the Christians driven back by the Moslems, grappling for survival. It never lost sight of the ascendency of the Visigoths or the stirring struggles in the Asturias. In the tenth century, Catalonia was thrown open to the strict influences of early Mediterranean Romanesque art which spread up the valleys of the Pyrenees. Further west, the triumphal road to Santiago acted as a conductor to all the influences of the West.

**Tahull: S Clemente**
Plan and analytical section 1:400

**Tahull: S Maria**
Plan 1:200

0 1     5      10      15   M
0   10    20        50   FT

0 1       5        10   M
0     10      20      30   FT

171

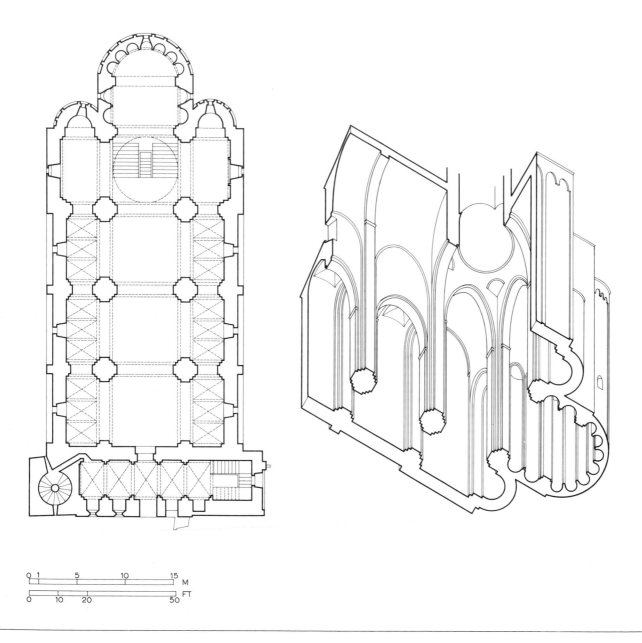

# 4. Unity of Vision

## An architecture suitable for times of war and calamity

Romanesque buildings may be on a grand or intimate scale, of expert or crude construction, fashioned either of well joined blocks or of common pebbles sunk in mortar, They range from lordly abbeys silhouetted against the sky to simple rustic sanctuaries conceived as separate entities. In all these cases, Romanesque architecture avoided the monotonous standardization of imperial Roman architecture, from which it claimed descent and which had spread across the world. The precarious background to existence, including war, famine and epidemics, and the ascendency of the feudal lords were enough to explain the almost complete absence of any preoccupation with large-scale town-planning comparable to the majestic schemes handed down by the ancient civilizations of East and West. In these disturbed times every inhabited area had first to be a defence and refuge.

The diminished cities regained the citadels and redoubts from which they had emerged under the Pax Romana. There are few aspects of history so significant as this return to earlier sites dictated by fear. Backed by the Pyrenees, the ruins of the Roman city of Lugdunum Convenarum cover a vast area completely unconnected with the site of the original town. Overrun by subsequent invasions the Roman city reverted to marshland and, later still, in the high Middle Ages, the bishops of St Bertrand de Comminges again established themselves on the restricted summit of the rocky hill. At Autun, the Roman city was built well away from the hill of Bibracte, the deserted site of the earlier town, and expanded over a larger area than that covered by the city today. As for the Christian city, it took refuge on the granite spur overlooking the plain below with its Gallic remains which, under the Empire, was no more than a setting for the massive Roman walls. Annecy in Savoy has an even stranger history. As a small Roman market town, its sole defence was the marshy ground bordering the mountain lake, and the settlement spread across the alluvial plain facing it. Later, its diminished population sought refuge on the nearby hill of Annecy-le-Vieux before deploying themselves for greater safety along the rocky slopes of the last outcrop of the Semnoz. Finally, the greatly expanded modern town again covered all these previously disputed areas.

## Unplanned towns

In the Romanesque world there were no longer any triumphal ways bordered by tombs, sumptuous buildings, propylaea, or arches to delight vain conquerors. It was not until the period of the decline of Romanesque civilization that new cities were created, and rediscovered the lost secrets of squares and the logical organization of space. Alongside these rational circular or rectangular plans, however, there long survived the mean districts and haphazard suburbs. Within Romanesque towns, picturesquely named streets, alleys and gutters, rather than noble avenues, formed a complicated maze. They were bordered by a confusion of buildings bearing no relation to any mathematical law, instead of by temples or proud mausolea. To the contemporary observer this chaos may seem to possess its own charm, but this is doubtless because it represents the attraction of what we ourselves have rejected. In Spain the famous route to Santiago drives straight through towns and suburbs which are crowded along its rough surface, but bear no relation to the road itself. At Cluny in the twelfth century, the rue d'Avril, probably the oldest street in the town, took the place of a triumphal avenue running in a straight line from the hills to the vast church. It winds, like an earthworm, between low, unaligned houses in the Romanesque tradition, with twin arcades of pointed arches at ground level surmounted by arcaded galleries.

As far as we can judge from the few examples left us, these muddled ground plans were balanced by a fantastic variation of roof lines also produced by an entire lack of a unified program. Right up to the Gothic age, old towns kept the outline of their indented roofs suddenly interrupted by the slender spires of church belfries. At San Gimignano in Italy social position was indicated by the height of the towers dominating the patrician houses. This childish rivalry between families caused the town to abound in these strange structures whose disconcerting irregularity and assymetrical perspectives are reminiscent of Manhattan skyscrapers.

On the burned, red peaks of Castile, the pink hills of Tuscany and Umbria, and the lunar plateaux of the Causses, the patina of eight centuries has succeeded in incorporating such silhouettes in the landscape, causing them to blend with the natural horizon. Originally, however, the violent brilliance of their gleaming white ramparts must have done just as much harm to the age old harmony of their setting as the large suburban blocks of today which pitilessly invade fields and woods.

This is not merely a surface connection or a transitory impression. The illogicalities of Romanesque, like those of modern architecture, had their standards, primarily determined by necessity and utility. Even the monastic buildings which multiplied throughout the Christian world did not succeed in avoiding them. The needs of austere monastic communities permitted many contradictory arrangements, and the regular stock plan with the church on the north side and a square cloister surrounded by the monastic buildings could be varied with reference either to the site or to the individual requirements of the institution. This inventiveness, however, was too common and systematic to be merely the result of unconscious necessity. It was also inspired by inherited taste.

## Unity with environment

History may have little to tell us about conditions pertaining to labor and workshops in the Romanesque period – this is something that does not become clear until the Gothic age – but there are signs that they were linked with the two complementary factors of materials and transport. Even before 1000, careful attention was paid to the geology of the soil both by the Benedictine monks and by simple country people. It was probably this sense of discovery that gave rise to the extraordinary knowledge of stone revealed by Romanesque craftsmen. Architecture descended from the lofty pedestal to which it had been raised by the false Carolingian renaissance and achieved a widely expanded diffusion. Stone was lovingly fondled and tested in all its reactions like a living, vibrating body. To the craftsmen it released the secrets of its color changes, its compactness, specific weight and elasticity. It becomes ever more obvious that all Romanesque investigations into spatial composition proceeded from this instinctive dispersion of knowledge which was no longer the jealously preserved perquisite of a single architect controlling an army of laborers. This may have caused Romanesque art to lose the imperious unity of mastery of technique. On the other hand, it gained a unity by its environment and a rich varied harvest of buildings.

## Organization of space according to simple rules

Romanesque masons were far from being theoreticians. Experience gained on the sites and detailed research are indicators of their sparing economy, absolute rejection of waste, practicality, and liking of security in preference to any form of expensive elaboration – all good 'peasant' virtues. To oversimplify a complex situation, every facet of Romanesque architecture brings us back to a few very simple rules: organisation of space into regular bays, and the juxtaposition or occasional superimposition of conventional masses arranged as interlocking cubes. Every advance in technical progress, whether the result of a migration of craftsmen, a detail seized by the quick eye of an architect, or a political conquest, was adapted to fit in with this schematic outline. Thus, military architecture profited from the Crusades by the discovery of the complex layouts and round sections of Byzantine fortifications. The old keeps of the eleventh century perched on their artificial mounds practically disappeared or were shut up behind a network of wards and casemates. Their construction involved the fitting together of a series of quadrangular spaces, which set far fewer problems than the building of the round towers of the retaining walls which must have contributed to the spread of domical vaults. Church building which was more detailed but less inventive, proceeded on the same basis.

It is no exaggeration to say that one finished bay is already a definite spatial unit, complete in itself. The rest is no more than a business of calculating simple figures which should not be forced into taking on too much symbolic value. We should do better to appreciate the spatial rhythm brought about by the succession of bays, like a ball which a group of players passes from one to another; for this is one of the richest, most evocative effects of Romanesque architecture. This interior movement, brought about by the balance of basic elements such as pillars and transverse arches, arcades and clerestory windows, is echoed by the exterior elevations punctuated by buttresses and lightened by bays and intermediary arcading.

## Independent bays with perfect or imperfect supports

These two categories are only seemingly contradictory. Recession and hollowing out make walls thinner and lighter as they get higher. Corbelling, on the other hand, causes the entire weight of a building to rest on a support diminished by the interplay of successive steps which submerge and divide internal pressures like the motion of invisible waves.

The efforts of Romanesque architects were concentrated on assuring the structural independence of the vaulted bay. The basic element was either led to independent organization by the interaction of carefully elaborated balances, or was assisted by external supports. So many different procedures and interior arrangements resulted from this choice that it would almost be possible to use them as a basis for a new system

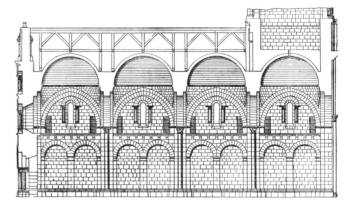

Gensac-la-Pallue (Charente): Church. Longitudinal section, showing the system of domed vaults.

Cross section: aisles with quadrant vaults.

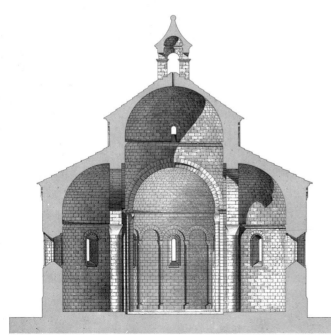

of classification for Romanesque architecture. The single naves, so suited to the demands of the liturgy (they were not divided by screens), had to make up for the absence of buttresses by a system of cloister or domical vaults which contained their own thrusts. Tunnel-vaults, on the other hand, required buttresses which could only be effective if they were applied to the probable breaking point or to the actual base of the vault. These conditions created quadrant-vaulted aisles, especially those which supported galleries so favored by the architects of Auvergne. Built after 1000 with the aid of rudimentary techniques, the narthex at Tournus turned out to be one of the most masterly constructions and one of the most powerful spatial combinations of all Romanesque architecture. At Cluny, less than a hundred years later, imperfect buttressing of the nave by the groined-vaulted aisles was avoided by doubling and staging them, thus containing the opposing counter-thrusts engendered by the pointed tunnel-vault of the nave itself.

## The architectural function of Romanesque decoration

To complete his task and bring a collection of dead

colors to life, a fresco painter takes up his brush and, with a few dazzling strokes, heightens the light on a face, emphasizes the fall of a drapery, or accentuates a contour. His work glows and is transfigured as if suddenly projected from the shadows. Just as with sketches, the technical construction of balanced masses lacks this final touch of genius.

In Romanesque architecture sculptured decoration assumes the important function of the final touch without which the most beautiful framework is no more than a dead skeleton. Like the painted decoration on the surface of an antique vase, it endows an apparently logical, functional structure with a touch of the irrational. From its barbarian and Byzantine ancestors the Romanesque world supposedly inherited a terror of empty space. Their architects had so strong a love of relief as an expression of the continual conflict between darkness and light that, even in some of their mural paintings, they tried with a subtle form of 'trompe-l'oeil' to imitate the barely perceptible flickering which agitates the surface of a mosaic.

The expedients peculiar to architecture halt at this frontier. The skeleton of a Romanesque church, as we have seen, only makes use of the simplest lines: staight lines, curves, circles and semi-circles. The schemes into which they are composed by the architect are plain and distinctive, invariably with a bias to the elementary. Variations are brought about by the precise details of adjustment. Yet, all can only be based on what happened when the creative artist was confronted with the object he either wished or was commissioned to portray. This last approach is, undoubtedly, a reversal of the traditional methods of archeological explanation. It is, however, the only method by which the diverse features of Romanesque art can be resolved into a single entity and by which one can distinguish between the artist's dreams and reality.

The large geographical areas which we have attempted to define as forming the background to this period of history also form the boundaries for different fields of Romanesque sculpture. From the late eleventh and in the twelfth century, they cease to be of absolute significance on account of wider migrations and exchanges; but the way in which the system of decoration was organized continued for a long time to reflect its distant origins. In the regions to the east of the Massif Central, it was never more

Tarascon (Bouches-du-Rhône): Ste Marthe. Door with sculptured cornice and arch moldings.

than a veneer, skilfully applied, but not really necessary. The fine Cluniac priory church at Paray-le-Monial, for instance, with its stiff ternary rhythm, is well suited to sparse ornamentation and gains from it a rather haughty dignity entirely suitable to its character. In the regions of the west, on the other hand, both ornamental and figurative sculptures are closely wedded to the churches. They adorn and help them to spring to life. The positions which they occupy, however, are only imperfect expressions of this spatial dualism which appears to have been pre-eminently based on religious needs.

## Positioning

It is surprising to find what a small part of the total surface of a Romanesque building was given over to sculptural decoration. The objective subordination of ornament is made clear by the fact that the architect almost always reserved it for the key points of the structure. If he broke the basic rule, balance was restored by compensatory influences. On exteriors, sculpture was limited to three well spaced features: cornices, arch moldings, and the tympana surmounting doorways. A cornice runs along the top of a wall below the fall of the roof which it stresses with its firm line. The corbels which support the ledge at intervals add a flickering effect. In eastern France they are usually plain, but, from Spain as far as Berry, they are decorated with tongues and scrolls, suggesting Arab influence. In western France these are found next to figured corbels, a system which gradually extended to the banks of the Loire. These small areas did not offer much scope to sculptors depicting men or animals. In some churches in Saintonge and Upper Auvergne, however, the ingenuity of artists, for whom no detail was of minor importance provided it played its part in the whole composition, endowed these small features with the entire range of their spirited imagination. Arch moldings have a twofold

function. They frame windows and doors with their curves and so serve to stress their structural roles. They also help to lighten the walls in which these apertures appear by a series of recessions and projections. By this means it was possible to avoid an ugly effect of coarsely scored stone. Usually, Romanesque sculptors reserved their skill for the archivolts of doorways whose large proportions were ill suited to being left bare, and limited the decoration of the smaller bays to discreetly molded keystones. In the West, however, and especially in Saintonge, they heaped decoration on them all, covering their surfaces with scrolls and palmettes or with small figures corresponding with the radiating axes.

These great sculptured portals proceeded from the unquestionable renaissance of the sculptor's art which, shortly before the twelfth century, completed the great architectural experiences of the eleventh and at the same time marked the result of all the continuous investigations since 1000. Their simultaneous appearance in Languedoc and Burgundy is proof of the scope of the development. The light, sober compositions of the Porte de Miègeville at St Sernin, Toulouse, and the west portal of the great church at Cluny give way to the frenzied apocalyptic visions and Last Judgments of the twelfth century. Gradually, sculpture achieved a fresher, richer and more mobile outline.

Attempts have been made to establish a connection between these great sculptured portals and the movement of pilgrims to Santiago. It is true that two of the most famous examples at Vézelay and St Gilles-du-Gard belong to shrines listed in the 'Pilgrims' Guide' as important stations on the road. Nevertheless, their almost total absence in Velay and Auvergne, despite the fact that these regions were traversed by many of these routes and were sanctified by the presence of many holy relics, very

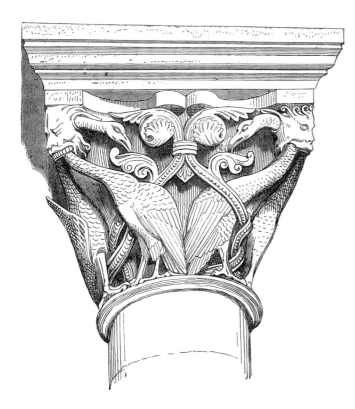

Déols, near Châteauroux (Indre): Church. Zoomorphic capital.

An example of the legends which inspired pious Christians.

much weakens this theory. Moreover, Poitou and Saintonge, though crossed by the western roads, offer no examples of this type. We may do better to take note of the geographical setting of these sculptures which must have been difficult to assemble. This invariably coincides with outcrops of limestone, a resistant material, easy to carve and cut up into large slabs, something which can hardly be said of the granite used for the churches of the Massif Central.

## The invention of historiated capitals

The latter region to some extent found compensation in the capitals surmounting pillars, which act as a break before the actual spring of the arch. This was a principle inherited by Romanesque architects from classical antiquity. They excluded the Doric and Ionic forms as having too little in common with their decorative ambitions but eagerly seized on the rich Corinthian variety reinterpreting it with the freedom of choice typical of their inventiveness. In the summer of 1964 a magnificent capital was retrieved from the site of the abbey church of Cluny: it probably came from the narthex constructed after the completion of the actual church about 1115 – 1120. With its elongated basket suddenly expanding into a powerful volute it provides a stylization of the Corinthian motif with a concentrated authority that may well remain unequalled. Early goldsmiths' work and pre-Romanesque illuminations, especially Irish, considerably enlarged the repertory with combinations of spiral and interlacing ornament as well as with zoomorphic decorations of monsters, back to back or facing one another, which were of Asiatic origin. Romanesque artists fully exploited the architectural function of capitals and, at the same time, completely recreated the details of their sculptured form. Their chief invention was to assign them an almost liturgical role by making them into illustrations of

Dijon : Abbey church of St Bénigne. Capital.

implied promise. The rules which these anonymous pioneers strove to formulate were those which were to continually engage the attention of later sculptors. Once again the creative process is clearly revealed at St Bénigne in Dijon. Almost all the capitals of the rotunda were undecorated except for those framing the west entrance which were adorned with strange, turbulent compositions in relief, one of which has been identified by André Parrot as the symbols of the four evangelists. It is difficult to realize that these compositions, examples of an already accomplished technique, are contemporary with the childish gropings expressed in some of the ambulatory capitals. With due

Aniane (Hérault): Cloister. Capital illustrating the agony of conscious sinners.

the wonderful stories on which the Christian faith is founded. Innumerable examples scattered throughout the Romanesque sphere of influence are moving illustrations of their ability to solve this dual problem successfully.

Two types of capital exist side by side. Each one crowning an isolated column is a complete entity. They are shaped either as truncated cones, or as cubes with their lower parts rounded off. When the column is reduced to a half-cylinder and forms a respond the capital is merely cut in half vertically and its profile remains unaltered.

These surfaces were suitable for leaf carving but were not as satisfactory as flat expanses for the representation of human forms. Plant sculpture on stone seems never to have died out, but the representation of human forms had not been attempted until the Romanesque sculptors boldly launched the attack. Their earliest efforts, dating from about 1000, are hesitant and unformed but also surprising on account of their

180

regard to the shape of the capital, an imaginative craftsman (ill-served by imperfect execution) has attempted to portray a figure in prayer. The roughly worked head has a low forehead vaguely imitated from Roman art with a long beard divided into two points by a center parting fitted between two clumsily raised arms. An unconvincing twist of the body causes the open palms to spread out to the corners of the capital which, elsewhere, are decorated with an abundance of elongated foliage. At the side the sculptor, either as a joke or as the result of an interruption, has left the sketched outline of his work inscribed on the surface of the stone – the furrow of the beard and the gesture of the raised arms. These glimpses of the capitals at Dijon are extremely valuable as they aptly sum up the basic principle of Romanesque sculpture: its absolute subjection to the shape and plan of supports, no matter how exacting these might be. This explains the anatomical deformations, excessive elongations and foreshortenings sometimes in combination, which so puzzled nineteenth century art historians. Romanesque sculptors hardly ever thought of imitating nature except in secondary details. Starting with an instinctive idea, they experimented with lines on stone, forcing a shape upon them, just as one looks for a profile or silhouette in a dissolving cloud. They were especially influenced by Irish illuminations, in which human bodies were twisted and bent into extraordinary attitudes. By means of bold foreshortenings, arabesques, distortions and baffling swarms of human shapes, the sculptors freed Romanesque architecture from its implacable logic, endowing it as if by magic with a sense of balance. The nearer this art approached technical maturity, the more it seemed to achieve a virtuosity essential to its needs. The scrolls and spirals of accomplished late works such as the wall at Charlieu with its agitated sculptures already showing signs of decline share the overwhelming spontaneity of the greatest frescoes.

Le Mas d'Agen (Lot-et-Garonne): Capital.

## The apologetic function of Romanesque decoration

There was much more to this technical development than a need to conform to stylistic requirements. From this whirlpool of shapes arose a single idea and a sense of direction which overran the world. This evolution finally resolved the dramatic tension between souls attracted to order and tranquillity and yet set in a cruel, inexplicable world. Romanesque architects peopled the earth with churches and chapels symbolizing eternity. Yet their sense of anguish and consciousness of sin invested these buildings with strange, unhappy monsters representing a melancholy, heartfelt appeal to redemption. This bestiary of monsters, which took such a hold on Romanesque imagination, represented far more than a reservoir of forms and decorative themes. It was a type of classification of a haunted, frightening world and its resources of evil. Everything there was linked in an infernal dance: nightmare animals, gryphons, monsters from the East, sciapods, dog-headed beasts and dwarfs with huge ears. They formed a strange picture of intellectual abandonment and sheer terror. The son of Adam was shown beaten, puny, doubled up on his bony knees, or involved in a pitiless hand to hand struggle.

Aix-en-Provence: Cathedral cloister. Angels guarding the Holy Sepulcher.

## Marked with the seal

Alone in the knowledge of their wretchedness, Christians were at least conscious of the rampart which sheltered them. Those blessed by God, the anointed prophets and saints who conquered the world, unmistakeably bore for its alleviation the signs of their election. They guard the sanctuaries with the angels who watch over the doors and oppose the fearful demon which holds out snares and torments; their gestures are solemn and their faces serene. We may choose our own favorites from the great gallery of Romanesque sculpture: the pensive Jeremiah at Moissac, Isaiah dancing at Souillac, the faces of the apostles with their fixed expression of reverence from the capital depicting the Last Supper at Issoire, the group of mourning women in the Easter dawn at Mozac, the wise virgins caught up in ecstasy at Civray, or the unfathomable foreboding of the Flight into Egypt at Autun.

The sculptors' tools were attempting, by concrete representation of the invisible world, to bring worshipers effortlessly to knowledge of it. Yet the sculptors were aware that the root of the formidable struggle lay in the immaterial world which was more real to them than the visible universe. The demons, symbols of the diverse power of evil which was to torture human souls by the express permission of God until the last day, occupied the sculptors' inmost thoughts and struggles. Lucifer, the very essence of evil, was seldom represented, probably out of panic fear and reverence, but his accursed children, the devils, occupied key positions everywhere. These dark images have no grandeur: the demons are ugly, vile and unclean, they can only inspire horror and physical repulsion.

## Spirits of light and triumph

Every Christian was aware that the man of sin, had to be revealed and that the Lord would consume and destroy him. The angels would be the ministers of his triumph. Thus, full of generosity and nobility, complete antitheses to the unclean spirits, they oppose their ordered majesty to the frenzied sculptures of the devils. Romanesque sculptors and the public to whom their message was addressed had a thorough knowledge of their categories as set out in the scripture. The Seraphim had three pairs of wings, one of which was to conceal the insupportable fire of the divine presence; in the tympanum at Perrecy-les-Forges these wings are used as a pretext for a double triangular composition which perfectly fills each zone on either side of the mandorla containing the seated figure of Christ. Usually, however, Romanesque iconography kept to the type, which had become traditional since the Ravenna mosaics, of magnificent young men richly dressed in long robes and splendid cloaks which blend with the harmonious curve; sometimes they wear military belts and carry on their backs a pair of widely spread wings. These legions are primarily revealed as the servants of God and his foremost worshipers. Every moment of every day, however, they were invisibly conducting a pitiless struggle against demons. Armed with sturdy swords which they flourished with heroic gestures, they protected themselves after the fashion of Frankish warriors, with oblong shields behind which mortal souls, portrayed as small, naked men, cowered for safety. Such military functions were suitable for angels. The Virtues who are found represented in frescoes at Les Allinges in Savoy and on capitals at Cluny were limited to contemplative and triumphal forms of worship.

The Archangels, who were held in the highest esteem by Christians of this period, reigned over this hierarchy. There were Rafael, the guide of Tobias; Gabriel, the messenger of the Annunciation; and, chief of them all, Michael, the sanctifier and illuminator of lofty sites where he had,

Vézelay: Abbey church. Christ in Majesty over the main portal.

without much difficulty, replaced the god Mercury. At Cluny, he was accorded a chapel high up on the inner side of the façade of the church; its small rounded apse overhung the nave, merely supported by a light system of corbels which can be seen developed at Payerne and the Cluniac church of Semur in Brionnais, a small marvel of late Romanesque. Michael features on the capitals of portals where he is shown overcoming the evil dragon, forbidding it entrance to the sanctuary. To the Romanesque soul, always conscious of pardon forcing mankind to repentance, this struggle did not represent the basis for a system of thought, but merely a fleeting moment of a period of trial. Romanesque sculptors, struck by the stirring

# Chronological Table

| | Historical Landmarks | Main Archeological Dates |
|---|---|---|
| 476 | End of the Roman Empire of the West | |
| 528 | Foundation of the Abbey of Monte Cassino by St Benedict of Nursia, reformer and legislator of western monasticism | |
| 800 | Re-establishment of the Empire of the West under Charlemagne | |
| 909 | Foundation of the Abbey of Cluny | |
| 936 | Otto I elected King of the Germans | |
| 941 | | Rebuilding of the east choir of the basilica of Agaune |
| 955 | Otto I's victory over the Hungarians at Lechfeld | |
| 957 | | Rebuilding of the church of Bañolas, Catalonia |
| 962 | Otto I crowned Emperor at Rome | |
| 987 | Hugh Capet elected King of France | |
| 994 | Odilo of Mercoeur elected Abbot of Cluny | During St Odilo's tenure as abbot: rebuilding of Charlieu, Souvigny, Romainmôtier, Payern (nave), etc. |
| 998 | Election of Pope Sylvester II (Gerbert of Aurillac) | |
| 1002 | Death of the Emperor Otto III | |
| 1003 | | According to Raoul Glaber, beginning of the general rebuilding of churches in the West |
| 1014 | | Consecration of the basilica of St Martin at Tours |
| 1015-1033 | | Building of the abbey church of St Michael, Hildesheim |
| 1030-1061 | | Building of Speyer cathedral |
| 1040 | | Consecration of the church of St Vincent, Cardona, Catalonia |
| 1041-1065 | | Building of the abbey church at Conques |
| 1049 | Hugh of Semur elected Abbot of Cluny | |
| 1062 | | Start of building of St Etienne, Nevers |

**Steps in Architectural Development**

| | |
|---|---|
| | 476 |
| | 528 |
| | 800 |
| | 909 |
| | 936 |
| First known example of an ambulatory with radial chapels | 941 |
| | 955 |
| First known example of a nave entirely vaulted in stone | 957 |
| | 962 |
| | 987 |
| | 994 |
| | 998 |
| | 1002 |
| The Comasini extend their influence to France: use of small stones, 'lombard bands' etc. | 1003 |
| First known example of pilgrimage type church – with unvaulted nave | 1014 |
| Transept with regular crossings | 1015-1033 |
| | 1030-1061 |
| Transept with dome on squinches over the crossing | 1040 |
| Prototype of 'pilgrimage road' church: nave with tunnel vault, buttressed by galleried aisles. | 1041-1065 |
| | 1049 |
| | 1062 |

| | Historical Landmarks | Main Archeological Dates |
|---|---|---|
| 1063 | | Building started at Pisa cathedral |
| 1066 | Norman conquest of England | |
| 1073 | Election of Pope Gregory VII | |
| 1080-1106 | | Rebuilding of Speyer cathedral |
| 1090 | | Work started on Ely cathedral |
| 1093 | | Work started on Durham cathedral |
| 1095 | Preaching of the first crusade | Pope Urban II consecrates the high altar of the new church at Cluny<br>Consecration of St Abondio, Como |
| 1097 | | Consecration of St Etienne of Nevers |
| 1100 | | Building of the cloister at Moissac c. 1100: Completion of the church of Anzy-le-Duc, pattern Vézelay |
| 1119 | | Consecration of the high altar of Cahors cathedral |
| 1120 | | Building of the nave of the abbey church at Vezelay<br>Start of rebuilding by the Crusaders of the castle of Saone in the Holy Land |
| 1130 | | Consecration of the new abbey church at Cluny |
| 1140 | | Consecration of the narthex of the new abbey church at St Denis |
| 1144 | | Consecration of the choir of the new abbey church at St Denis |
| 1146 | Preaching of the second crusade | |
| 1147 | | Consecration of the Cistercian abbey church at Fontenay |
| 1152 | Death of Suger | |
| 1153 | Death of St Bernard, Abbot of Clairvaux | |
| 1156 | Death of Peter the Venerable, Abbot of Cluny | |
| 1163 | | Work started on Notre-Dame, Paris |

## Steps in Architectural Development

|  |  |
|---|---|
|  | 1063 |
|  | 1066 |
|  | 1073 |
| Adoption of groin vaults for naves (cf. 1100: Anzy-le-Duc) | 1080-1106 |
|  | 1090 |
| First known example of a choir roofed by a rib vault | 1093 |
| General use of round-headed arches and cylindrical vaults | 1095 |
| Perfected type of Romanesque Church with developed plan and systematized vaulting. Direct lighting of naves and galleried aisles. | 1097 |
| Nave completely roofed with groin vaults | 1100 |
| Church vaulted with a series of domes (type of Souillac, Solignac, Fontevrault, etc.) | 1119 |
| Adoption of circular towers derived from Byzantine military architecture | 1120 |
|  | 1130 |
|  | 1140 |
| Start of Gothic architecture: stained glass, rib-vaults | 1144 |
|  | 1146 |
|  | 1147 |
|  | 1152 |
|  | 1153 |
|  | 1156 |
|  | 1163 |

kaleidoscope of the Apocalypse, and dependent on the architect, only made use of the scenes of triumph. The theme of the beast attacking the woman crowned with stars representing the sufferings of the Church militant is never found depicted inside churches.

## The changeless summit of the pyramid

Transcending these agitated storms and the chaotic whirlpool of human and celestial battles is the firm dominating keystone on which the entire structure depends from the lowest foundations to the summit of the tower—the Son of God. He reigns supreme from the tympanum of the portal to the frescoed semi-dome of the apse where he is represented in majesty in a riot of blue and crimson. Representations of Christ enduring the Passion which every Christian must share are few. At Montceaux-l'Étoile in Brionnais, however, he is shown as victor over death still holding the instrument of torture and, at Conques, it is held at arm's length by two angels. The Cross may also be seen outlined behind the Christ in glory at Beaulieu. Greater stress was put on the episodes in which the Son of God bears witness to his humanity which were continually celebrated by the theologians and preachers of the eleventh century with Odilo of Cluny at their head. Later on, themes relating to the childhood of Christ expressed the development of religious enquiry and the evident humanization of Romanesque iconography. Scenes of the Nativity, the Adoration of the Magi, and the Flight into Egypt, which continually excite Christian fervor, are found next to representations of the Annunciation and the Visitation. Amid these shines the gentle beauty of the face of the Virgin, mother and queen, to whom Romanesque artists always responded, even before the time of St Bernard. Before winning pride of place in the tympana of Gothic cathedrals, she sits with the Apostles contemplating the radiance of her son's Ascension with an indefinable sadness.

The bond of theology links the commemoration of the Last Supper with this day of separation from mankind. The image of the sacrificial Lamb fulfils its purpose in the dream of Revelation. Risen from the prophetic depths it is worshipped by the patriarchs and sometimes, as at Charlieu, accompanies the risen Lord who shares the chief position in Romanesque tympana with the Christ of the second coming. The visionary artists set the Son of God in triumph in the center of a mandorla, the glorious oval which, at Conques, is scattered with stars. The figure of Christ is surrounded by the symbols of the Evangelists, often amazingly portrayed, and, at Moissac, the terrible majesty of his face transfixes the spectator and seems to summon him by name from the beginning to the end of time. The continuity of the Romanesque vision reaches its final achievement with the compelling sight of the end of the world engulfed in its own tumult.

At this point we may more readily appreciate the strange lack of proportion between the religious buildings on which the Romanesque genius concentrated its creative vitality, and the few surviving examples of secular architecture produced by the same workshops. It appears perfectly clear that the final explanation of this basic reality is not contained in any technical, geographical, historical or archeological factors, but rests in the depths of souls sustained and inhabited by the breath of God.

# Bibliography

In many ways this book is complementary to my recent study **'Pelerins du Moyen Age'** (Paris, Fayard, 1963, Collection Résurrection du Passé). More particularly it expands the third part in which I attempted to explain one of the most difficult and exciting problems facing the historian of Romanesque architecture: the extent of the influence brought to bear by these migrations and mass groupings on the general economics and religious significance of contemporary buildings. It is also a summary of a series of lectures on art history given over several years at the University of Lyons. This caused me to formulate a method of investigation which is perhaps best described as 'total archeology,' having recourse to the full range of history, geography, local customs, philosophy and theology. For this reason it is difficult to specify and enumerate all my sources.

The bibliography of the Romanesque covers a vast field, and a review of all the works I have consulted would fill a second book. The best account of the development of Romanesque architecture and its different forms is **'Carolingian and Romanesque architecture (800-1200),'** Penguin Books, 1959 (Pelican History of Art) by the American professor, Kenneth John Conant. This book contains a full bibliography. Almost as exhaustive is Pierre Lavedan's **'Histoire de l'art. Moyen Age et Temps modernes,'** 1944 (Paris, P.U.F., Collection Clio). This is only slightly out of date and sets out the problems of Romanesque art extremely clearly. Its bibliography includes works which are now classics such as Viollet-le-Duc's **'Dictionnaire raisonné de l'architecture francaise du XIe au XVIe siècle,'** Dehio and Bezold's **'Die kirchliche Baukunst des Abendlandes'** and the massive **'Histoire de l'art'** edited by André Michel and still in use (Vols I and II, Paris, 1905-6). In addition, there are the specialized periodicals which have analyzed and discussed the achievements of the Romanesque for a century or more. These include the French **'Bulletin Monumental'** and **'Congrès archéologiques,'** the **'Journal of the British Archaeological Association'** and the American **'Speculum.'** Finally, there are more recent works such as Henri Focillon's brilliant **'Art d'Occident'** based on his contribution to the **'Histoire de la civilisation occidentale au Moyen Age du XIe au milieu du XVe siècle'** (in collaboration with Henri Pirenne and Gustave Cohen, Paris, P.U.F., 1933, Collection Glotz).

Studies of individual regions are just as numerous and only the chief ones can be listed here. For France there are Camille Enlart's fundamental **'Manuel d'archéologie française'** (I: Architecture religieuse, II: Architecture civile et militaire. III: Costume. Paris, Picard, 3rd

189

edition revized, 1927) and Robert de Lasteyrie's **'L'architecture religieuse en France a l'époque romane'** (2nd edition revized and enlarged by Marcel Aubert, Paris, 1929). England is covered by A. W. Claphan's two brilliant studies: **'English Romanesque Architecture before the Conquest,'** Oxford, 1930, and **'English Romanesque Architecture after the Conquest,'** Ibid. 1934, and by Sydney Toy's **'The Castles of Great Britain,'** London, 1953. The German Empire by E. Hempel's **'Geschichte der deutschen Baukunst,'** Munich, 1949, and Louis Grodecki's **'Au seuil de l'art roman. L'architecture ottonienne,'** Paris, 1958. With regard to Italy, Venturi's **'Storia dell'arte italiana,'** Milan, 1904, is supplemented by Mario Salmi's **'L'art italien,'** Florence, 1953, **'L'architecture romane de Toscane,'** Milan and Rome, 1927, and **'Eglises romanes de Toscane,'** Paris, 1961. G. Rivoira's **'Le origini della architettura lombarda e delle sue principali derivazioni nei passi d'Oltr'Alpe,'** Milan, 1908, refers to the 'maestri comacini.' There are also A. K. Porter's **'Lombard architecture,'** New Haven, 1915-17, and E. Arslan's **'L'architettura del 568 al mille'** from **'Storia di Milano,'** Vol. II, Milan, 1954. Finally, for Spain we have L. Torres Balbas' **'El arte de la alta edad media y del periodo romanico in Espana,'** 1934, and, on the problems of early Romanesque art, Puig i Cadafalch's three invaluable studies: **'L'arquitectura románica a Catalunya,'** Barcelona, 1908-18, **'La geografia els origens del primer art romanic,'** Barcelona, 1932, and **'Le premier art roman,'** Paris, 1928.

Since the end of the Second World War, many illustrated publications have appeared whose main purpose has been to familiarize a wider public with Romanesque buildings and art treasures. The most important have been those put out by Editions Braun. Those so far published are – J. Gantner and M. Pobé: **'L'art monumental roman en France,'** 1955; H. Decker: **'L'art roman en Italie,'** 1958; M. Durliat: **'L'art roman en Espagne,'** 1962, and H. Busch: **'L'art roman du Saint-Empire,'** 1963.

We must also include the Editions Zodiaque (La Pierre-qui-vire, Yonne), publishers of the series **'La nuit des temps.'** 12 out of the 21 volumes are wholly devoted to French Romanesque art: Burgundy, Auvergne, Val de Loire, Poitou, Touraine, Roussillon, Anjou, Quercy, Limousin, Angoumois, Forez-Velay, and Rouergue. More recent publications include one on Romanesque art in Switzerland, one on the buildings of the Crusaders in the Holy Land, and two volumes devoted to Catalonia. Romanesque art is also largely represented in Dimier's book on Cistercian art and Françoise Henry's three volumes devoted to Irish art.

The photographs of the castle of Saone, in Syria, on pages 152, 153 and 154, have been supplied by M. Gerard Zimmermann, and the aerial view of the same building, on page 155, is from the French Institute of Archaeology in Beirut.

M. Gerard Zimmermann, of the Institute of the History of Medieval Art, at Geneva, was also responsible for the documentation for all illustrations in the text.

190

# Table of Contents

3 **The Heritage of Romanesque Genius**
by Hermann Baur
7 The Approaches
7 A Legacy threatened and betrayed
10 An ambiguous resurrection
11 Prosper Mérimée
11 Viollet-le-Duc, theorist and prophet
13 An ambiguous definition
14 Birth of the Romanesque World
17 **Captions for plates 21-44**
20 **Notes**

47 **1. Background to Romanesque**
47 From darkness to dawn. The last invasions of the tenth century
49 The turning point of 1140
Suger and the light of the Gothic
50 The Council of Sens, outlet of the mystique of the Romanesque
51 A slow but irresistible transfer
52 Cluny, motive force of Romanesque civilization
53 An apogee of building history
54 The trend towards a new asceticism
54 The emergence of Capetian France
55 Youth of the Romanesque World
57 The theory of 'schools'
58 Communication
59 The 'churches of the pilgrimage roads'
59 Churches with series of domes
60 Monastic patrons, first in the field of reconstruction
61 Splendor and light of the great Romanesque churches
62 Church treasuries and ornaments
63 **Captions for plates 67-82**
66 **Notes**

85 **2. The Builders**
85 Popular needs
87 Architects or mere masons?
89 Some names on the stone
90 'Gislebertus hoc fecit'
91 Cluny
92 Saint-Benoît-sur-Loire
93 The Cathedral of Compostela
93 Glory to God through assembled stones

94 A symbolic architecture: the circular plan
97 Churches with series of domes
99 From asceticism and denial to total architecture: Fontenay
101 **Captions for plates 105-124**
104 **Notes**

127 **3. Impulses and Themes**
127 The progress of dissemination
128 The Ottonian center
128 Development of transepts
129 'Composition of masses'
130 Prelude to the Romanesque
132 Beyond the frontiers of the Empire
133 Normandy and England
134 The Architects of Como
135 Catalonia
136 The spread of the Mediterranean forms of early Romanesque art
137 From Burgundy to Provence
137 The Centers of Aquitaine
138 Auvergne
140 Western France
142 Atlantic Spain
143 **Captions for plates 147-170**
146 **Notes**

173 **4. Unity of Vision**
173 An architecture suitable for times of war and calamity
174 Unplanned towns
175 Unity with environment
175 Organization of space according to simple rules
176 Independent bays with perfect or imperfect supports
176 The architectural function of Romanesque decoration
178 Positioning
179 The invention of historiated capitals
181 The apologetic function of Romanesque decoration
182 Marked with the seal
182 Spirits of light and triumph
184 The changeless summit of the pyramid

**Plans**
18 Vignory: Church
19 Angoulême: Cathedral
19 Fontevrault: Abbey kitchens
45 Poitiers: Notre-Dame-la-Grande
46 Tournus: St Philibert
64 Conques: Ste Foy
65 Nevers: St Etienne

83 Fontenay : Abbey
84 Payerne : Abbey Church
102 Almenno S Bartolomeo : S Tomaso
102 Tuscania : S Pietro
103 Portonovo : Abbey church of S Maria
125 Alpirsbach : Abbey
126 Maria-Laach : Abbey church
144 Ely : Cathedral
144 Castle Hedingham, Essex
145 Saone, Syria : Castle
171 Tahull : S Clemente
171 Tahull : S Maria
172 Cardona : S Vicente

78–82 **Payerne :** Abbey church
105–107 **Almenno S Bartolomeo :** S Tomaso in Lemine
108–111 **Tuscania :** S Pietro
112–115 **Portonovo :** S Maria
116–117 **Monteriggioni**
118–120 **Alpirsbach :** Abbey
121–124 **Maria-Laach :** Abbey church
147–149 **Ely Cathedral**
150–151 **Castle Hedingham**
152–155 **Saone :** Castle
156–159 **Tahull :** S Maria
160–163 **Tahull :** S Clemente
164–168 **Cordona :** S Vicente
169–170 **Estella :** Romanesque House
Jacket : **Fontenay :** Abbey Cloister

185–188 **Chronological Table**

189–190 **Bibliography**

## Plans accompanying text

9 Abbey of Cluny
12 Vézelay : Abbey church
15 Map of the West
48 Tours : St Martin
49 Diagonal rib vault
50 St Pol-de-Leon : Church
52 Cluny : Abbey church of SS Peter and Paul
52 Lewes : Priory
54 Cistercian abbey of Senanque
56 Jerusalem : Church of the Holy Sepulcher
88 La-Charité-sur-Loire : Church ambulatory
89 Moissac : Cloister
91 Cluny : Abbey church of SS Peter and Paul
92 Saint-Benoit-sur-Loire : Abbey church
94 Santiago de Compostela : Cathedral
96 St Michel d'Entraigues : Church
129 Hildesheim, Germany : St Michael
130 Speyer : Cathedral
131 Merseburg, Germany : Cathedral
132 St Benoit-sur-Loire : Abbey church and Caen : Abbaye-aux-Hommes
139 Clermont-Ferrand : Notre-Dame du Port
139 Orcival : Notre-Dame du Port
176 Gensac-La-Pallue : Church
177 Tarascon : Ste Marthe
183 Vézelay : Abbey church

## Plates

21–23 **Vignory :** Church
24–27 **Angoulême :** Cathedral
28–32 **Fontevrault :** Abbey kitchens
33–36 **Poitiers :** Notre-Dame-la-Grande
37–44 **Tournus :** St Philibert
67–70 **Conques :** Abbey church of Ste Foy
71–73 **Nevers :** St Etienne
74–77 **Fontenay :** Abbey